Printed in the USA

Bipolar Disorder:
35 Outside of the Box Tips To Manage Bipolar Disorder

By James Skolski

Contents

Introduction

Bipolar disorder, also known as bipolar affective disorder, is by no means an easy disease to live with. It can have many negative or adverse effects and lead to distressing symptoms such as mood swings, depression, and, in more serious cases, self-harm. Bipolar disorder is often associated with mood swings, which lead to a state known as manic depression. There are two modes of this depression, split between depression (the lows) and mania (the highs). Mania leads to people to be very excited, and sometimes show outbursts of either over-the-top happiness or extreme energy. The other side, depression, can be characterized by bouts of sluggishness, reduced eye contact, isolation as well as a negative outlook on the world. In addition to these ailments, bipolar disorder can also be very problematic when being treated. This is because, in many cases, traditional medicine is not successful in effectively treating bipolar disorder. In order to help this, the following sections of this guide will cover many alternative or lesser-known treatments that can be helpful at dealing with symptoms commonly associated with bipolar disorder.

While finding a good treatment for bipolar disorder can be tricky, there are several alternative options that anyone suffering from bipolar disorder can explore. These techniques and alternative practices fall into a large array of categories, ranging from physical practices to the more mental. Each one of these allows different ways to combat the disorder, and most help combat different ailments as well.

In each sections of this guide, we will explore the effects of bipolar disorder, both associated with mania and depression, and then look at what causes such symptoms. Then, we will cover certain types of alternative treatments, and see which one helps with what symptom. In this way, we will not only explore each treatment, but have an in depth look at why such treatments are used as well as how they can be used to their most effective level.

Before we begin, there is one very important overarching rule to understand. Although there are many treatments laid out in the following pages, you always want to find a practice that works best for you. Not every treatment helps with each part of the disease, and it is always best to target specific symptoms rather than trying to tackle everything all at once. Doing your own research, and knowing what works best for your body, are some of the most important aspects of dealing with any disorder. This approach will give you the best results, and enable these alternative treatments to work as well as they can.

Though they are all different and help in different ways, each treatment in the following pages will be gone over in a very similar way. One important thing to know, most treatments, whether it is medicinal or more unconventional, are going to have certain side effects. These side effects can range from minor to some of the more serious. This depends largely on what type of treatment you are using, and how extreme that treatment is. Knowing these side effects is very important due to the way we will cover alternative methods for treating bipolar disorder. First, we will look at and discuss exactly what each method is. Then, after the overview, each practice will be explained in the way it applies to helping with bipolar disorder. This includes which specific symptoms each treatment applies to as well. Then, the setbacks of each treatment will be explained in order to help understand the risks that each one can have. This will tie each treatment together and give you a proper understanding of which individual treatments are best for you.

The causes of bipolar disorder are largely speculative, but that does not mean the treatments are. The following pages, if followed and understood, will be helpful for anyone trying to deal with bipolar disorder. While not every method we discuss will be used for treating bipolar disorder specifically, they all will attack symptoms of bipolar disorder (such as depression or anxiety). The effects of bipolar disorder may be detrimental if left untreated, but they can be handled if you take the proper measures. It may is a very difficult disease to live with, but rising above it is most definitely possible. It just takes some research, some work, and a little patience. There is no cure for bipolar disorder, but does that doesn't mean it cannot be helped.

BIPOLAR DISORDER:
35 OUTSIDE OF THE BOX TIPS TO MANAGE BIPOLAR DISORDER

1. Acupuncture

The first type of alternative therapy we will cover in this guide is one of the more daunting: acupuncture. On the whole, people tend to shy away from acupuncture as a treatment for many different disorders and diseases. Research shows this is largely due to two reasons. One, little is known about acupuncture as a process, and awareness of it is very slim. Two, because the awareness about this method is so slim, there are many who do not trust acupuncture as a reliable treatment method. However, if used correctly, acupuncture can be a great way to treat or help with a wide range of different disorders. Bipolar disorder happens to be one of them.

When you strip down acupuncture to its base values, it is about centering the body's energy. Many Chinese practices are based on this idea of energy, and its importance to your overall health. If your energy is flowing correctly, chances are you will be in a better space both physically and mentally. However, if your flow is thrown off, it can lead to problems. By using acupuncture, you can set your energy flow in the right direction, which will then lead to you leading a healthier life.

To ensure you have a good flow of energy, acupuncture targets strategic points across your body. These points, which are often referred to as acupoints, are what help balance the energy's flow. These acupoints are each located on a certain meridian, or specific channels of energy flow. By inserting needles into these meridians, which change depending on what type of energy you are trying to reset, you can re-balance the energy of your body. This works because each meridians is a point in your body that, when stimulated, help stimulate nerves, muscles and connective tissue. This re-balancing has been shown to have many positive effects, such as a reduction in physical discomfort and mental illness, as well.

Acupuncture is most commonly used as a way to stimulate your body's natural painkillers. As a result, it is a great way to naturally fight against pain. While this can be very beneficial, in terms of bipolar disorder, acupuncture is most commonly used to treat the onset of depression. Depression, in combination with the highs and lows of the disorder, is one of the most forefront problems associated with bipolar disorder. Offsetting this can be very useful, and a good way to help stabilize your mood. In fact, a decrease in depression has been commonly seen in patients using acupuncture as a form of therapy. This is most likely due to the fact that acupuncture releases endorphins, the chemicals that control feelings of pleasure or happiness in the body, when used.

Many mood-stabilizers stimulate endorphins as a way to fight depression. Acupuncture works in this way as well by stimulating the bodies neurotransmitters. A neurotransmitters, which will be referenced many times in the following sections, is defined as a chemical substance that is released at the end of a nerve fiber by the arrival of a nerve impulse. These are what help control your brain. As a result, they also have a large effect on your mood, and if you have high levels of positive chemicals, such as β-endorphin, or the monoamines (such as serotonin and noradrenaline) it can be very good for your mental health. Not only that, but these neurotransmitters can also lead to a more positive mood as well.

In addition to helping your mood, acupuncture can help with many other ailments you may be experiencing. If you are suffering from nausea or pain, it can be used to reduce those problems. Acupuncture, through its natural healing ability, has also been used to treat many types of physical pain, such as lower back pain, headaches and migraines. In terms of mental problems, acupuncture can also be used as a way to help deal with anxiety for many of the same reasons it is so effective at dealing with depression.

One thing to remember, acupuncture, though effective, does have its share of risks. However, these can easily be avoided by being aware. Just like with any type of medical help, you want to find an acupuncturist that is best for you. There are many fields of acupuncture, and it is always smart to get help from someone who specializes in treating the specific ailments you need to treat. This way you will make sure you have access to the best and most focused care possible.

In addition to making sure you are seeing a proper physician, it is also a good idea to be aware of some of the side effects that can occur when using acupuncture. As you are using needles, there is a chance of bleeding or bruising. Much of this is natural, and should not be worried about. However, if you are pregnant, have a pacemaker or suffer from a blood disorder, it may be best to avoid using acupuncture altogether as it can create problems for anyone who falls into the above categories. Acupuncture can cause extra bleeding in those with blood disorders, and some types of acupuncture use small electric pulses, which can affect a pacemaker's ability to work. There is also a small chance that the needles can injure organs or tissues, which is something you want to be aware of. The most important rule is, when using this method, always listen to your body. If something hurts, you see extra bleeding or an aspect of the treatment doesn't feel right, it may be a good idea to take a break and look for other methods listed in this guide.

Sources: *Qureshi et al., Neuropsychiatric Disease and Treatment. 2013; 9:639*

Ernst et al., Int J Risk Saf Med. 1995; 6:179

BIPOLAR DISORDER:

35 OUTSIDE OF THE BOX TIPS TO MANAGE BIPOLAR DISORDER

2. Amino Acids

There are many different kinds of medication used in the treatment of bipolar disorder. These medications come in many forms, and this section of the guide will look at one specific form, supplements. Supplements help to naturally allow your body to regulate itself in a healthy way. The supplements that will be covered in this section, which are amino acid supplements, help specifically by allowing the stimulation of certain chemicals. These chemicals can have positive effects on your mood as well as your mind, and each one will be explained below.

Many negative aspects of any disorder stem from a certain deficiency happening inside the body. Thos with bipolar disorder commonly experience amino acid deficiency. One of these acids is tryptophan. Tryptophan has long been thought to be a precursor to endorphin stimulators, such as 5-hydroxytryptophan and serotonin. These stimulators are needed for a positive mood, as discussed in the above section As such, low levels of tryptophan have been linked to lower levels of these stimulators, which in turn leads to a more depressed state. Tryptophan also stimulates serotoninergic neurotransmission through "precursor loading", which also has been known to offset symptoms of depression. If you are suffering from low levels of tryptophan, it is suggested to take 50-200 milligrams as divided dose.

Though tryptophan is very beneficial when it comes to mood stimulation, there are a few side effects, though minor, that are worth noting. Dry mouth is a common side effect associated with tryptophan use. A state of sedation can also come with using this acid. Finally, intestinal distress has also been associated with tryptophan. However, these effects are relatively minor in comparison to the benefits of using it to boost your mood.

N-Acetyl Cysteine (NAC) is another amino acid that has a great deal of positive benefits. Just as tryptophan serves as a precursor to serotonin,

NAC is derived from the amino acid cysteine, which serves as a precursor to glutathione. Glutathione is a very important antioxidant in your brain, and having proper levels of it can lead to many similar benefits as having high levels of serotonin or other neurotransmitters. In this way, NAC, due to the way it triggers such reactions, enables more control over both mania and depression. Through this control, it also can improve the overall quality of life. This was seen in a study (*Ravindran et al., Journal of Affective Disorders. 2013; 150:707*) whose results showed the positive effects of NAC on the brain of those living with bipolar disorder. The results of this study also showed the way NAC can help boost moods, and that it works best when used in conjunction with more traditional mood stabilizers.

When looking at amino acids that help with the effects of bipolar disorder, there are two more that should be considered. The first of these is Phenylalanine, a naturally occurring amino acid that can be found in some foods. It is mostly used as a way to fight both pain and depression. However, when using it as a way to stabilize mood, you should be aware of some of the side effects. These can range from constipation and fatigue to heartburn and headache. Still, if you do find that Phenylalanine works for you, it is generally suggested to start off by taking 500 milligrams a day. Then, once this becomes normal and your body adjusts to the higher levels, this can be increased to 3 to 4 grams a day.

The last amino acid that will be looked at in this section, taurine, is noted here due to its calming effect. These calming effects are very important as they are one way you can stabilize mood. For this reason, a lack of taurine has been linked to an increase of mania. As such, if you taking taurine supplements, it can help with the offsetting of mania symptoms.

Taking each of these amino acids can lead to its own pros and side effects. You should be aware of each of these when choosing to use supplements. Doing your own research, as covered, is very important in finding what treatment works the best for you. Always be aware of what is going into your body, and understand what amino acid will affect you in the most positive way.

Sources: *Ravindran et al., Journal of Affective Disorders. 2013; 150:707*
Lakhan et al., Nutrition Journal. 2008; 7:1
Qureshi et al. Neuropsychiatric Disease and Treatment. 2013; 9:639

BIPOLAR DISORDER:
35 OUTSIDE OF THE BOX TIPS TO MANAGE BIPOLAR DISORDER

3. Aromatherapy

The next alternative method in this guide is one of the more unusual practices we will cover, and that is the use of aromatherapy. Aromatherapy, as its name implies, is using your sense of smell, or an array of different smells, as a way to bring positive aspects to both your body and mind. Aromatherapy has many positive effects that directly help with ailments that have been associated with bipolar disorder, which is the reason that it can be such an effective form of treatment. Aromatherapy, refers to the practice of breathing in the scents of certain oils. Each of these oils has different properties, and each property has some type of positive effect associated with it. While these different types of oils have a wide range of effects, this section will be more centered on the broader benefits that can come from aromatherapy.

Plants have been used for medicinal purposes for hundreds of years, and aromatherapy is one of these purposes. Before we begin with the explanation, it should be noted that, as with any treatments, there are certain risks associated with aromatherapy. These are heavily dependant on your individual health as well as medical history. It is always a good idea to consult your physician in addition to performing your own research before starting aromatherapy practices.

Aromatherapy has been noted as beneficial to those with bipolar disorder due to its ability to affect mood. The regulation of mood, which can help balance out both depression and mania, will be at the center of many practices in this guide. Aromatherapy is no different, and its calming effects can yield great results. Aromatherapy, when used correctly, stimulates the pleasure centers of the brain by way of the nerves in the nose that sense smell. This connection lead to overall better moods, which improves the overall quality of life. It also helps by effecting an array of hormones and enzymes in your blood. Additionally, it has also been linked to the simulation of the adrenal glands. In this way, aromatherapy has a plethora of benefits, which also includes to helping distress that can trigger problems in mood disorders, such as depression and anxiety.

There a various kinds of aromatherapy, and each of them has potential benefits. One such method is massage aromatherapy, which incorporates massages with the breathing of the oils. This creates a calming sensation in the physical body as well, and has been show to lower anxiety. This method can even curb depression or symptoms of depression. It is not commonly used as a way to treat the more severe types of depression, but can be beneficial when serving as a way to lessen the more mild types. In this way, it can be a good way to try and overcome some of the lows experienced with bipolar disorder. There are many ailments that aromatherapy can help combat, but for the purposes of this guide, we will only be looking at the ways it can help increase mood.

As stated earlier, there are some risks associated with aromatherapy that you want to be aware of. The most important factor is to understand how to properly use the oils. Never get them in your mouth or ingest them, as this can cause serious health risks. In addition, understand some oils can be harmful when applied onto skin, causing burning or rash. When applying oils to skin, you never want to apply too much, as this is more likely to lead to burning. This burning during over-application is most commonly seen in eucalyptus, bergamote and peppermint. Vapors released during the aromatherapy process have also been known to irritate the eyes. There is also a chance of many common medicinal side effects such as nausea, headaches, drowsiness and agitation.

Just as with any medicine, you want to be vigilant when using aromatherapy. Always know the side effects, and deal with them as they occur. Every practice laid out in this guide can be good when used to its fullest potential, but also comes with risks. Aromatherapy is no exception. However, if you want a safe, alternative way to help with treating distress, which can come in the form of anxiety or depression, it is a great way to go. There are plenty of different oils available, but only some that center on areas related to those effects of distress. If you are aware of which ones you need and the best, safest way apply them, aromatherapy can be one of the more effective treatments at fighting negative aspects of bipolar disorder.

Sources: *Andreescu et al., Journal of Affective Disorders. 2008; 110:16*

BIPOLAR DISORDER:
35 OUTSIDE OF THE BOX TIPS TO MANAGE BIPOLAR DISORDER

4. Art Therapy

Treatment and methods commonly used to help with bipolar disorder come in many different forms and methods. As in the above sections, that can be the power of smell or assorted supplements. However, there are also more unconventional ways of thinking. Often, these unconventional forms have been shown to have great results in helping people combat negative aspects of bipolar disorder. The one we will look at in this section, which is both quirky and effective, is the power of art.

Art therapy is a method of treatment that acts as a form of expression. Through this expression, patients are able to get into better touch with themselves and the problems they are facing. The American Art Therapy Association defines this treatment as "a mental health profession in which clients, facilitated by the art therapist, use art media, the creative process, and the resulting artwork to explore their feelings, reconcile emotional conflicts, foster self awareness, manage behavior and addictions, develop social skills, improve reality orientation, reduce anxiety, and increase self-esteem". This reflect the goals of this type of practice.

Just as with traditional therapy, art therapy is a way that allows patients to overcome their own emotional conflicts. However, instead of predominantly talking, the patients create art to express how they feel. This expression has been linked to a number of different benefits, which range from improved mood and better self awareness to reduced anxiety and higher self-esteem. These attributes are especially important in fighting depression as well as both negative thoughts and feelings.

Another reason art therapy can be so effective is, many times it is hard for people with disorders to properly express themselves. This lack of expression can come from many different avenues, but allowing patients to overcome that lack of expression is very liberating. Art is a space where they can create, where someone can be who they are and truly show how they are feeling. As the art is usually a reflection of mood or a person's attitude, it can be easily looked at by a working therapist. The therapist then examines the art and seeks to better understand the patient through their work. Often times, this leads to the patient improving in their mood as well as their mental health.

One such example of this was with a woman, who will be called Mrs. Robinson. Ms. Robinson was a 78 year old woman admitted to a nursing home due to her bipolar 1 disorder. This change made her often agitated, and she suffered from bouts of extreme anger. While most of the traditional methods and medicines were shown to have no effect on her, Ms. Robinson was very responsive to art therapy. In the therapy, while she never spoke or interacted with her therapists, her art saw a trend over time. This trend was a shift towards a happier and more positive outlook on life. When treatment first began, Ms. Robinson's paintings were scattered, angry and dark. However, by engaging in art therapy, they eventually became brighter in conjunction with her mood. After four weeks of these therapy sessions, she was discharged from the facility.

The above example is only one story, but it does show the great effects that art therapy can have in helping with bipolar disorder. Self-expression is very key in having a healthy mind, as it promotes a level of self-control that is not normally seen in everyday life. This sense of control directly affects self esteem, which has been shown to become boosted with repeated art therapy sessions.

Using art therapy as a method of treatment for people with bipolar disorder has also been shown to give patients a better understanding of their own problems. The art, or the act of creating said art, gives patients time to reflect on their own lives. It also gives them a space where they can be alone with their thoughts and feelings. This itself is a type of therapy, which can be helpful to those who need it. Just like with self-control, this reflection can be used as a way to stimulate mood and cut back on signs associated with anxiety or depression.

The overall goal of art therapy is to improve or restore a client's functioning and his or her sense of personal well-being. It does this through the practices outlined above. If you seek to use art therapy, you want to do so in an environment where you feel most comfortable. The overall goal of this therapy is to improve or restore your functioning and sense of personal well-being. The type of art being created doesn't matter, as long as they are creating something worthwhile. If you are taking part in art therapy, just create something that works for you, whether it reflects your mood, your attitude, or simply how you're feeling on that particular day.

Though many tests have been done on the benefits of art therapy on those with different disorders (which includes bipolar disorder), no side effects have been seen from the treatment. Since art therapy is a non-invasive practice, and since nothing is being taken into your body, it makes sense that this is one of the most risk free treatments you will find in this guide. All you need is some paper and a pen.

5. Ayurveda

Ayurveda is next method we will look at for helping with bipolar disorder. For those that do not know, Ayurveda is a term that refers to a type of Hindu traditionalist medicine. This medicine puts a stress on a connection between mental and physical ideas, and is an alternative method whose effects can be linked with helping bipolar patients improve their overall quality of life. In order to understand how Ayurveda works, it is best to know that it is split into two, distinct parts. The first of these is the body, that is enriching the physical form, and the second is the mind or mentality, which is especially important in dealing with problems that arise from bipolar disorder.

Bipolar disorder is a very daunting disease, but it can be overcome. This idea is at the heart of Ayurveda, which bring benefits through a "balancing" of the body and mind. This is very similar to the way that acupuncture balances the channels of the body, but instead of using needles, you use an array of different methods. Herbs, in addition to diet and lifestyle changes, are all examples of the methods used. Each of these has effects that will help improve your lifestyle through physical and mental channels.

Ayurveda is very dependent on your body having a balanced state. This balance is central to wellness, and the wellness that comes from Ayurveda cannot happen without it. This stems from an ancient line of thinking that enables you to find the best way to help you. In this line of thinking, each person has a set of three different principles of body and mind which are called Vata, Pitta and Kapha.. These principles are called "doshas". Each "dosha" is unique to each person, and using the herbs and changes outlined below, you can help to correctly balance your own doshas. This is important, because having unbalanced doshas can lead to numerous problems. These imbalances come from misuses of the body, such as a lack of exercise.

At its base, the thinking behind Ayurveda is very good in helping curb symptoms of depression. As depression is one of the more prevalent effects from bipolar disorder, it is easy to see how using this method to fight depression can be so beneficial. However, in addition to this effect, Ayurveda can also be very good for people who are not doing well with their prescribed medication. Medicine has been found to have certain effects on the body, with side effects being a normal part of today's world. These side effects can be particularly strong in treatments for bipolar disorder. If you are not doing well with traditional pills or treatments, it may be a good idea to look into using the herbs and changes associated with Ayurveda. This is because, many of the medicinal herbs used in this treatment are traditionally better tolerated by people than traditional types of medication.

In a study (*Qureshi et al., Neuropsychiatric Disease and Treatment. 2013; 9:639*) it was shown that Ayurveda has many benefits associated with helping symptoms of bipolar disorder. The diagnosis of which is based on a comprehensive history, detailed physical examination, measurement of vital signs including pulse, and relevant laboratory tests. However, results from tests associated with Ayurveda have been inconclusive at times. This is commonly due to the fact that most results are based on a certain person rather than a larger group. Additionally, these types of herbs can also be slow when it comes to altering or effecting moods, but this is commonly seen in most herbal treatments used for mood disorders. However, this is slightly different when it comes to Ayurveda, as the herbs in this treatment have much greater effects on mood. Small preliminary studies of major depression treated with herbs, herbal mixtures, and Rasayanas (a special branch of Ayurveda aiming to rejuvenate and nourish the body at all levels and comprises several products manufactured from a combination of herbs) have demonstrated improvement in depression scores.

Clinical depression is one of the forefront problems associated with bipolar disorder. As this depression is not always effectively battled with traditional drugs, Ayurveda, the changes to lifestyle in addition to the herbal supplements, can be a very productive alternative form of treatment. When choosing to use Ayurveda as a way to treat mental disorders, you always want to be aware of is what types of herbs you are choosing to use. As with aromatherapy, understand the importance of doing your own research in addition to consulting professionals. This is because, some instances of Ayurveda have been seen to have harmful metals or chemicals in them. This lacing can have large, negative repercussions on your health. Not all herbs contain these toxic substances, however. If you understand and figure out the healthiest options associated with Ayurveda, you will be fine.

Sources: *Qureshi et al., Neuropsychiatric Disease and Treatment. 2013; 9:639*

6. Choline

Lecithin, also known at phosphatidyl choline, is a phospholipid that is generally found in foods that are high in fat. It helps improve memory, and is also important to certain brain processes. In those with bipolar disorder, lecithin has also been linked to helping with mood stabilization. The subject of this next section, choline, is one of the active ingredients in lecithin, that can be found in a wide range of foods, spanning from eggs to spinach to chicken.. Choline is an essential nutrient that is found in most living tissue. It is important for many molecular functions, most notably the transferring of lipids and intracellular signaling. Due to this, choline deficiencies can be very problematic, and tend to have negative effects on your health. Taking choline supplements can remedy these deficiencies, and they can also aid with other detriments of bipolar disorder.

Perhaps the most important function of this compound is its role in intracellular signaling, or the way cells interact with each other. Choline plays a role in this because it is a constituent of acetylcholine, and acetylcholine is needed for this signaling process to happen. While it does have its share of side effects, which will be covered in greater detail below, choline can be very beneficial for many functions, especially when taken as a supplement.

If you are seeing a deficiency in choline levels, it is best to take 10-30 grams as phosphatidyl form in divided doses. This treatment specifically helps with mania above all other symptoms. This includes the range of manic symptoms as well, such as aggression, euphoria, poor judgment and rapid speech. It is also good at reducing levels of hypomania. It may also be helpful by improving or increasing the efficiency of brain energetics. In many neuropsychiatric disorders, including bipolar disorder, these energetics are commonly damaged through things such as inflammation. Choline can help to repair this damage. It can also be useful in helping with erections as well. If you want to take choline, it can be purchased, and can also be taken with food. It is also 100% natural, which in itself can have certain benefits to being used over more mainstream medicine.

However, despite the potential benefits of choline when dealing with bipolar disorder, there are some setbacks associated with taking extra supplements. Choline can increase your overall body temperature, which can lead to sweating. Nausea, one of the more common side effects of bipolar treatments, can also occur along with a loss of appetite.

Despite it's effects, choline's use in the treatment of bipolar disorder is still in its early stages. As such, there are only a few studies that have looked at how it works. Still, due to lecithin's benefits to those with bipolar disorder, there is no reason to think that choline would be any different. Many treatments help with depressive symptoms, but due to its effects on the brain, if you are having problems with mania, or if you are experiencing high levels of hypomania, this may be a good supplement to go with.

Sources: *Lakhan et al., Nutrition Journal. 2008; 7:1*

7. Chronotherapy, Sleep Deprivation and Melatonin

Chronotherapy, one of the more peculiar methods in this guide, is a practice that refers to the shifting of your sleep schedule. It may seem odd to alter or shift your sleep schedule, especially when trying to deal with a mental disorder. However, while this is generally true, it has many benefits when it comes to helping those suffering from symptoms of bipolar disorder. The main one of these benefits, as with so many treatments, is acting as a proficient mood stabilizer. Here, we will look at how the shifting of sleep schedules, in addition to other factors of chronotherapy, can help regulate mood, and how that regulation of mood creates a better life overall.

When shifting your sleep time in accordance with chronotherapy, there are several ways to do it. You could sleep either earlier or later, less or more. Each shift will be different based on the person, but this form of therapy simply connotes a change to your normal sleeping habits. By shifting these habits, you set a rigid schedule that will help you conform to the new way of sleeping. Creating this new schedule will help in two different ways. One, it has been found to create a strict control of the sleep-wake cycle. Two, it also has been shown to create a certain control over the light-dark rhythms. Each of these have shown to allow for better moods in bipolar patients, and they have also been shown to have mood stabilizing effects. However, this will only be effective when control over the sleep schedule is achieved. Putting yourself into a tight, rigid schedule will give you the necessary control that you need.

When trying to implement a certain type of sleep schedule, it may be beneficial to take medication that will help you fall asleep. There are many options for this, but melatonin is one of the most effective. Melatonin, chemically known as N-acetyl-5-methoxytryptamine, is a naturally occurring hormone that helps regulate the light-dark cycle in living organisms. This is why it can be such an effective sleep aid. When you are trying to create a new sleep cycle, aids such as melatonin can be very effective at helping you fall sleep at a certain time. If you do take melatonin, which is ingested orally through either capsules, tablets, or liquid, it is best to take it 3-6 milligrams. This can also be useful for people suffering from melatonin deficiency as well. This medication is best taken around 9 pm.

Another important element chronotheraputic treatment is sleep deprivation. Just as with the shifting of your sleeping schedule, actively taking part is sleep deprivation can have some less-than-desired results. However, these effects, which will be covered later, can be worth it if chronotherapy or sleep deprivation is found to help your mental health. Sleep deprivation is a process that has been seen to help those suffering from depression. Depression caused from bipolar disorder can have some negative effects, and though it might seem strange, choosing to not sleep can reverse some of these negativities.

When using sleep deprivation, it is best to start slow before taking shorter and shorter periods of sleep. There are two types of sleep deprivation, and both can be effective at battling depression. The first of these is partial sleep deprivation. Here, the patient doesn't avoid sleep, but rather just only sleeps for short periods every night. These periods usually last around 3 to 4 hours, and acts as a way to still get some rest while losing sleep. The other, and more extreme, method of sleep deprivation is total sleep deprivation. In this method, the patient simply avoids sleep for long periods of time. Here, sleep avoidance can last days, going as long as 40 hours.

While not sleeping for 40 hours can put strains on your body, to minimize the risks of sleep deprivation, each awake period is followed by what is called a recovery sleep. That is a longer period of sleep, which gives your body a chance to rest. The results of sleep deprivation in this manner have been recorded through numerous trials as well as small studies (*Ravindran et al., Journal of Affective Disorders. 2013; 150:707*).

Researchers have found that sleep deprivation has mullti-modal influences on mood, involving impact on thyroid hormone levels. In addition, it has also been found to have effects on metabolic and monoaminergic functioning as well. All of these benefits, in addition to curbing depression, were noted more in people suffering from bipolar disorder who underwent the treatment than those not suffering from the disorder.

As taking part in sleep deprivation can cause added stress or fatigue to your body, there are some side effects from using this method. Most are minimal, but all focus on the toll the treatment can have. These effects are headache, fatigue, gastrointestinal symptoms, sleepiness, and worsening of depression or hypomania in vulnerable patients. Some of these may be uncomfortable, but, as previously stated, it is always a good idea to use treatments that work best for you. Every method is going to have some ramifications, but if you can manage to find one that helps your symptoms, then that is the one you should use.

Sources: *Ravindran et al., Journal of Affective Disorders. 2013; 150:707*

8. Color Therapy

Unlike the above methods and practices, the next form of treatment has no real side effects. Some forms of treatment, especially for those who do not want to take or have trouble with all forms of medicine, are meant to try and help you through bipolar disorder without having to use pills. These forms can range in both form and efficiency. The one that will be covered in this section is color therapy.

Color therapy is very similar to chronotherapy in that is a non-invasive way of treating bipolar disorder. However, instead of trying to use your sleep cycle as a form of therapy, this uses colors. The ideas behind this therapy are centered around the human body's natural response to certain colors. It is an inherent fact that all colors, warm or cold, bright or dark, have some type of effect on your psyche. This effect then triggers a certain response in your nervous system and mind. These responses are what color therapy is based off of.

When seeking to combat the effects of bipolar disorder without medicine, color therapy is a relatively simple process to choose that has minimal backlash. For this reason, it can be extremely useful to people who find it to be effective. When using color therapy, you want to change the colors of things in your life or your regular environment. Doing this can help with mood stabilization, as changing these colors are a great way to improve or regulate your mood.

The most important part of color therapy is knowing which colors can illicit which moods. Not every color will make you feel the way that you want to feel. As such, it is important to figure out which method is best for you. For example, the colors green, violet, pink and blue have a peaceful, soothing effect on your mind. These are best used for relaxation. Other colors, like red, can create more passionate or powerful responses. Darker colors, like black and purple, allow calming effects, where orange can build feelings of success.

Once you know how different colors can help your mood, incorporate those colors into your normal, everyday life. Being around objects that stabilize mood is one of the most important aspects of this treatment, and exposure to them will help you feel the way you desire. If you need to be more passionate, make sure the items in your life are red, if you want to be calm, try to use blues or greens. This is especially important in two different spaces of your life. One space if your home. Having certain colors in your home can help the space feel more comfortable and relaxing. This will help you be at ease and regulate your mood in your a space where you should feel safe. The second space where color is important is at work. If you find a certain color helps stabilize you, you should find a way to incorporate it into your space at work. This can be done by using decorations or simple ornaments. If you do not work in a space that can be decorated, you can also dress in the color that helps you.

Clothing is a very important part of life, and, through the power of color, can help stabilize your mood. Clothing is very good for this, because it is something you always have on you and is constantly in your immediate environment. As it is always present, clothing color therapy is recommended for keeping you level-headed and reasonable in your work environment. This kind of constant exposure to a certain color can also help keep manic symptoms down in addition to other benefits.

Color therapy is a great form of alternative medication. Know that there are many different type of medication-free treatments available to those battling with bipolar disorder. Color therapy is not only a good method that provides no side effects, but it also very easy to implement. Merely buying or finding items that are an array of certain colors is the only thing you need to implement this practice. Since this type of therapy is also done on your own, it is one of the few methods that you can do with no outside sources. The only thing you need is a knowledge of colors, the way they make you feel, and learn which ones are best for helping your personal symptoms.

9. Dark Therapy

This next section will cover a type of treatment that is very similar to chronotherapy. However, instead of inducing long periods of sleep, this therapy, which is commonly known as dark therapy, uses long periods of darkness as a way to help with bipolar disorder. This practice is especially beneficial at helping patients with bouts of mania.

Just like chronotherapy, dark therapy tries to fight bipolar disorder through controlling both the wake-sleep cycle as well as the light-dark rhythms. At the center of this treatment is the therapeutic benefits of being submerged in total darkness. The time of this differs, but it is common to be exposed to 14 hours of enforced darkness. This, once again as with chronotherapy, is juxtaposed with a rest. The rest usually happens for 14 hours, most commonly from 6 p.m to 8 a.m.

Dark therapy can be very helpful for numerous reasons. The first of these is because it helps with melatonin stimulation. People with bipolar disorder can have abnormalities with melatonin secretion, which can hurt the amount of sleep they get. In addition, bipolar disorder patients have also shown greater sensitivity to the effect of light. This is one of the main reasons that dark therapy can be so extremely effective when helping with mania and other bipolar-related symptoms. Unmonitored exposure to artificial light and sleep disruption, due to the multiple types of environmental stimuli, could act as triggering factors for mood episodes in bipolar patients. This type of treatment is another way to enact control over the wake–sleep and light–dark rhythms, which in turns help stabilize moods.

Dark therapy is built around two distinct parts. The first of these is actually invoking a more restful sleep, which allows for better sleep at night. This increase of sleep can have many benefits, which will covered below. The other part is helping regulate mood through a set exposure to light. As light can trigger certain responses in those with bipolar disorder, controlling when that exposure happens can aid those effects as well.

One study (*Barbini et al., Bipolar Disorders. 2005; 7:98*) looked at the how exactly dark therapy could be helpful specifically to those with bipolar disorder. In this study, researchers looked at 32 patients affected by the disorder. The patients then combined dark therapy with their regular treatments. Analysis was taken over a two week time, where those undergoing dark therapy using 14 hour cycles of darkness. After the results were compiled, it was found that the treatment was very successful in helping deal with as well as control mania. This was largely due to the reasons discussed in the above paragraphs. Furthermore, patients who used traditional medicine in conjunction with dark therapy slept better than those who only used medicine. This is a strong indicator of how effective dark therapy can be at inducing better sleep.

Sleep loss, or restlessness during sleep can bring about many unhealthy symptoms. By controlling the light-dark cycle, it is easier to overcome these negative effects. When dark therapy is implemented, other symptoms, such as mood swings, also lessen as well. Dark therapy is not something that typically used alone, but it can be very effective when used with other types of treatment; especially some of the more traditional bipolar medications such as lithium. In recent years, the combination of sleep–wake rhythm manipulations, antidepressant drugs, light therapy, and lithium have provided clinicians with new instruments to achieve rapid and sustained antidepressant responses. All of these are not necessary to make dark therapy work successfully, but it is a good example of how it can be used to its fullest potential.

Though it may be surprising, there are no real side effects that have been associated with dark therapy. Being prolonged to darkness may seem like it could have negative ramifications, but since this type of treatment is based around sleep, this is not the case. If you are having problems dealing with mania, dark therapy can be a very strong way to fight this. Also, if you are having trouble sleeping, or if a lack of sleep is giving you other problems that bleed into your life, this can be a good solution. When using dark therapy, just remember it is not a treatment to use on its own.

Sources: *Barbini et al., Bipolar Disorders. 2005; 7:98*

10. Diet

As with so many other treatments, diet has been shown to have a large effect on bipolar disorder. Having a certain diet can be very beneficial at battling symptoms. The diet that will be discussed here, which can be used by those with bipolar disorder, is what is called a ketogenic diet. A ketogenic diet, like any diet, involves shifting what you eat. However, a ketogenic diet is unique in that it attempts to force certain tissues in the body to change their primary fuel source. The brain is one of these tissues, which is why it can be used as a way to treat disorders that are centered around the brain, such as bipolar disorder. A ketogenic diet can also be significant in that it can alter nerve activity, which is thought to have calming or relaxing effects. These effects can also reduce distress that can worsen bipolar disorder.

A ketogenic diet revolves around minimizing the intake of carbohydrates while taking in high levels of fat while also taking in adequate levels of protein. This will help achieve the goal of the diet, which is to maintain a starving or fasting metabolism over an extended period of time. Using this process removes glucose from your diet. As a result, when glucose from digested carbohydrates becomes absent, your liver then makes ketone bodies from partially-burned fatty acids. This is how this diet then switches the fuel your body uses. The ketones that are created from your liver are remnants of fatty acids. These remnants are secreted into the bloodstream, and are used as fuel for the brain in place of the glucose that you are no longer ingesting.

Once there is an increase in ketones in the brain, it affects amino acid metabolism. This refers to an increase of the amino acid glutamic acid into a different form, known as gamma-aminobutryic acid, of GABA. High levels of GABA production makes nerve cells much less excitable, which is how it helps control certain functions in the body.

Though it has been more focused as a treatment for children with epilepsy, the ketogenic diet's effect may also be good for people with bipolar disorder. One reason for this, is the diet itself has been seen to be effective at helping raise the seizure threshold, which is why it can be used as a treatment for epilepsy. What does a seizure threshold have to do with bipolar disorder? While those with bipolar disorder do not commonly experience seizures, many of the treatments for bipolar disorder also raise the seizure threshold. These can range from things such as anticonvulsant medication to electroconvulsive therapy. As such, it then stands to reason that, because of this correlation, a ketogenic diet's effects will also be a good way to help with bipolar disorder.

As a result of the aforementioned link, ketogenic diets may help stabilize those with bipolar disorder, and allow them better control over their moods. The reasons behind this are unknown, and is not know what the therapeutic effects of the ketogenic diet ate. It could simply be the presence of ketone bodies in the blood, but it also could be the stabilization of blood sugar levels. These benefits could also stem from the reduction in blood sugar and insulin levels, or some combination of these that give the user positive benefits while undergoing this dietary shift.

We will now look at a study to further analyze the effects of the ketogenic diet when helping treat bipolar disorder. This study came out in 2013, and was published in the magazine "Nuerocase". In it, two women who were both diagnosed with type 2 bipolar disorder, which is a subset of the disorder with greater bouts of depression and less mania, ate diets that consisted of mainly meats. These meats were beef, seafood, chicken and pork. They also stuck to fattier foods, such as oil and cream. They each continued this diet for 2 to 3 years, and in both cases the women saw positive results. Mood stabilization was greatly improved, and each women had little to no adverse effect. This is another example of the benefits a ketogenic diet can have.

While the above study saw little adverse effects on the women, that is not to say the ketogenic diet should not be used without caution. Changing your regular diet, in any capacity, can have effects on your body. When first starting the ketogenic diet, many people can experience bouts of sluggishness or fatigue. This is normal, but may be more pronounced here. There are numerous other side effects you may experience as well. On the minor side are many small irritants, such as constipation, dehydration, and electrolyte or micronutrient deficiencies. However, the ketogenic diet can have some more serious complications as well. These more serious problems are things such as kidney stones and high cholesterol. Bone fractures and gall bladder problems can also occur. As such, always be vigilant when undergoing this diet, and know that caution is key.

11. EEG Biofeedback

Moving on from changes in diet, we will look at another method that attempts to help with symptoms of bipolar disorder by making alterations to the brain. In this case, the method is electroencephalogram (EEG) biofeedback therapy. EEG is also known as neurofeedback, and it can be very beneficial to those with bipolar disorder. This is because EEG has been found to affect all different parts of the brain, which can help with things such as mood stabilization among other problems that affect people with bipolar disorder.

Neurotherapy has been shown to be very effective in treating a wide range of mental disorders. This process works by using sensors on the scalp which measure EEG frequencies. The reading of these frequencies allows real-time feedback, which can be either video or audio, that rewards frequencies associated with relaxed attention, and suppressed frequencies commonly associated with under-or-over-arousal. The overall goal of EEG is to develop skills to enable the self-regulation of brain activity. In this way, those with bipolar disorder can help regulate their mood swings while also better regulating bouts of both mania and depression. Because this method rewards responses tied to relaxation, this helps creates calming sensations within the brain, which then translates to the body.

Most of the data compiled on the effectiveness has been tested in children. However, there is some evidence to also suggest that the benefits of EEG translate to adults as well. This also goes for the treating of bipolar disorder using EEG. Only minimal feedback has been compiled so far, but due to its effectiveness with other types of disorders, the application of EEG seems reasonable and effective. Not only that, but since EEG is commonly used as a way to help change functions in the brain, which is a common element of many bipolar disorder treatments, there seems to be no reason why this method would not be effective. In fact, in the small number of trials conducted studying EEG's effect on bipolar disorder, it has been seen to give positive results to those living with bipolar disorder.

EEG is a process where patients learn to produce certain brain wave patterns. These patterns are usually associated with positivity and other beneficial results. The basis of this is simply learning how to think in a certain way, much how you would learn any new skill. Neurofeedback takes this to the next level by giving you access to methods and feedback that were previously unavailable to you. This system works by "rewarding" you when you think in a certain way. Every half second, you brain activity is compared to your targets for change. When you meet the goal, whatever it may be, you get a signal and a "reward". When you do not achieve the goal, you do not receive the reward. This system enables you to help mold your mind to the way that you want.

Due to the lack of overall trials, if you want to use neurofeedback to help with the effects of bipolar disorder, it is recommended to discuss it with your healthcare provider first. However, the negative effects do not go beyond that. The lack of research, or rather that this treatment is still in the early testing stages, is the only real setback about this practice. For the most part, neurofeedback has many benefits over some other methods of treatment. This is because it is easy to do, easy to learn while also being non-invasive.

One last note on EEG, is that it is not a practice you do by itself. While some of the methods in this guide, such as acupuncture or chronotherapy, may yield great results when used independently of other methods, neurotherapy is not one of those methods. EEG, in the limited tests and results that have been performed, only really works when combined with other treatments, be they medicine or other types of therapy. If you want to use neurotherapy to help curb your symptoms, make sure you keep doing you other treatments just as you normally would. If you are taking medicine or supplements, continue to do so, and if you are undergoing some other form of therapy, keep your scheduled time. EEG, when treating the effects of bipolar disorder, is not something you need to alter your lifestyle for.

12. Electroconvulsive Therapy

Electroconvulsive therapy, which is a treatment that uses electrical shocks to treat undesirable or negative symptoms, is another method that can be beneficial when finding ways to cope with bipolar disorder. While a bit off-putting, this method can actually help with many difficult symptoms that come with general bipolar disorder, such as mania and depression. While this does not strictly act as a mood stabilizer, electroconvulsive therapy (also known at ETC) can be very helpful in improving how one lives with the disease.

During electroconvulsive therapy, electrical currents pass through the through the brain, which triggers positive responses in the body. In this way, this helps you overcome many of the common problems of bipolar disorder. The goal of this procedure is to help mania or depression by changing chemicals in the brain. Bipolar disorder is caused largely by imbalances in the brain, which is why it causes a shifting of moods. By passing a current through the brain, the hope is that the electricity will jostle the brain and cause a seizure. Do no worry, this seizure is relatively harmless, and when the electrical current is fed through the brain, the patient is always under a general anesthetic to prevent any harm. However, the seizure is strong enough to change the brain's chemistry. This alteration of the brain chemistry is what will lead to the alteration of certain moods or help with certain disorders.

Since the brain of a bipolar patient, in its current state, is experiencing problems, changing that function will result in a more positive chemistry. ETC, while used for the broader symptoms we discussed above, is particularly useful for those who suffer from some of the more extreme conditions, such as suicidal thoughts or symptoms associated with psychosis. However, electroconvulsive therapy has a wide range, and has been found to be effective in over 75% of all cases.

ETC is most often used for fast relief from either mania or depression, and also works in a relatively short amount of time. Overall, electroconvulsive therapy is most often brought in when many traditional methods, such as medicine or other doctor-regulated therapies, fail to work. If a patient is not responsive to a certain type of medicine, or if they simply cannot handle the necessary dosage, then ETC may be a good alternative.

Electroconvulsive therapy is, despite what you may think, a relatively safe procedure. In addition to the anesthetic, people who undergo ETC also are given a muscle relaxant. This ensure that the seizure only applies to their extremities, such as hand and feet, and won't cause any bodily harm. In addition, the patient is very carefully monitored during the treatment to make sure that nothing goes wrong. ETC is relatively short, and the patient, after the shocks are sent to their brain, awakes a few minutes after the treatment finishes. They may be slightly confused, but besides that confusion, they have no recollection of what they just went through.

Beyond the more severe treatments that ETC helps with, it can also be a good way to treat acute mania in addition to more extreme signs of depression. However, discuss the possibility of ETC with your doctor for any number of symptoms. This is because, since the success rate of electroconvulsive therapy is so high, chances are it is at least worth asking about if you are suffering from something that you cannot quite overcome with medicine. In terms of treatment times and schedule, electroconvulsive therapy is most commonly given three times a week, and this lasts for two to four weeks. As aforementioned, the tests are usually pretty short.

As expected, there are a number of side effects that come from this therapy. However, that does not diminish how effective this type of treatment can be, nor does this diminish exactly how safe this procedure is when compared to other treatments for bipolar disorder. In fact, most of the risks labeled here (or that are found in conjunction with ETC) are more due to the anesthesia than the actual treatment. The most common side effect of this treatment is short-term memory loss. This usually goes away one to two weeks after treatment. This can also be mitigated based on how the electrodes are placed on the scalp, and other aspects of the procedure. Confusion and nausea (once again most likely a result of the anesthetic) are common side effects as well. ETC can also cause headache and jaw pain in some isolated cases. However, once again, these are very minor irritations when compared to the success rates associated with electroconvulsive therapy.

Sources: *Loo et al., Journal of Affective Disorders. 2011; 132:1*

13. Exercise

Every treatment we have covered so far has been focused on using shifts or alterations of the mind to help with symptoms caused by bipolar disorder. This next section, while still a very good treatment, will look at the other part of the equation: your body. It is an inherent medical fact that the brain and body are linked. This connection works both ways. That is, a healthy body leads to a healthy mind and vice versa. This thinking can be applied to the treatment of bipolar disorder through the use of exercise. Exercise is one of the best ways to build your body, and keeping your body healthy, due to the connection to your mind, can also help deal with bipolar disorder.

Time and time again, exercise has been proven to have positive effects on mental health. In addition, it has also been found to yield benefits associated with boosted self-esteem, a sounder sleep, as well as better attitude about yourself. One of the most important aspects of battling bipolar disorder is keeping a healthy lifestyle. While this applies to things such as eating well, reducing stress and getting enough sleep, it also applies to getting a good amount of exercise. The Depression and Bipolar Support Alliance (DBSA) has stated that exercise is a good way to keep mood swings at bay. In addition, through the results on its effect on mania are unclear, regular exercise has also been shown to help with depression brought on by bipolar disorder.

Cardiovascular exercise, that is exercises associated with the heart, such as running or walking, have been found to be more effective than weight training when it comes to bipolar disorder. Aerobic exercise, when done either vigorously or routinely, have also been shown to increase sleep. As we have covered in some of the above treatments, sleep, especially in relation to both the light-dark cycles, is very important to helping those with bipolar disorder.

In order to make your workout as effective as possible, it is best to create a set cycle with which you can depend on. It is most commonly suggested by the National Sleep Foundation, that you workout more vigorously in the morning, and save easier, or lighter workouts (which can include things such as yoga) for the time before you bed. This will allow you to get the best sleep possible, which will then increase the amount of overall benefits that come from exercise.

When actually planning your workout schedule, the Depression and Bipolar Support Alliance (DBSA) recommends a long-term exercise goal of 30 minutes a day. While this does not have to happen every day, you should try to exercise at least 3 days a week. It should be noted that, more so than many other treatments in this guide, it is best to consult your doctor before starting a workout program. It is common for those with bipolar disorder to have very delicate stages of health. As such, it is best to set up a plan, as well as a style of workout, that your doctor suggests is best for you. This will help you minimize any other problems or health risks that come from exercising.

When starting an exercise program, you should start out slow. After getting into a routine, you can then work up to a healthy intensity. This will help you get into the proper rhythm. One of the biggest challenges those with bipolar disorder face when it comes to exercise, is sticking with a schedule. Schedules can be very difficult for those with bipolar disorder to keep. However, there are some things you can do to stick with a routine exercise program.

The first of these methods is to pick a form of exercise that you enjoy. Doing anything you find enjoyable is one of the key ways to make sure you continue doing it. If you find there is an exercise that you find yourself not liking, switch to one you like more. Starting slow will also make the exercising process much easier, which will make the feeling of accomplishment much higher. If you can enhance this feeling, it will keep you coming back. The last way to make sure you stick with your workout plan is the use of a partner. Working out with another person can be helpful for many people, and it may also act as a good source of social interaction. However, it is important to make sure the person you workout with is someone who brings calm, rather than stress, into your life.

In terms of side effects, researchers say that the type of exercise you do related to the mood determines if it is helpful or harmful. For example, if you are in a manic state, then calming exercises would be more helpful, as they would not exacerbate the symptoms. This is because vigorous exercise may elevate activation. In addition, patients on certain medication, such as lithium, should stay well hydrated during their workout. Any form of dehydration while on these type of medicines can increase their levels of toxicity.

Having a healthy body leads to a healthy mind. This is very true of exercise, which has been shown to have anti-depressant as well as mood-stabilizing effects. It can also be used to help treat symptoms of anxiety, low self-esteem, and addictions that can also affect bipolar patients. Exercise can also help with maintaining a healthy weight and getting better sleep. All of these factors are especially key in the lives of those with bipolar disorder in that they all also reduce mood swings.

Sources: *Wright et al., Journal of Affective Disorders. 2012; 136:634*

14. Folic Acid

For this next section, we will revisit the idea of supplements as a way to effectively treat symptoms commonly associated with bipolar disorder. Once again, we will focus on one specific type of supplement that can have some very powerful benefits. This is folic acid. Folic acid is a water-soluble derivative of vitamin B. Folate, which acts as another form of vitamin B, is found naturally in food. It has many health benefits, and can be very important for some basic bodily functions. Folic acid is a form of synthesized folate, which is how it can be taken in supplement or pill form. Folic has acid has also been added to many different types of food since 1998, including many diet staples like cold cereals, flour, bread, pasta, bakery items, cookies and crackers. However, folate also occurs naturally in a wide range of different foods. It is commonly found in leafy greens (spinach, broccoli, lettuce), okra, asparagus, fruits (bananas, lemons, melons), yeast, mushrooms, orange and tomato juice as well as meat (beef liver and kidney).

Folic acid is used as a way to treat many different diseases and health-related issues. It can be helpful when dealing with bipolar disorder, because folic acid is needed for the body to properly develop and function. Folic acid is also needed for the proper synthesis of DNA as well as other bodily functions.

One of the main reasons one would take folic acid to is to combat a folate deficiency. Folate deficiencies happen across all different types of people, but is something that has been seen in people who experience bipolar disorder. People with bipolar disorder commonly have low levels of folate, which can have effects on their body. As such, if you combat those low levels with folic acid, it can help fight back against some of the symptoms. In terms of dosing, if you do take folic acid to battle a folate deficiency, of if you find it works very well for any ailments your experiencing, it is recommended to take 200 milligrams a day. This will make sure you get the proper dosage you need in order to foster a more complete life. This is backed up by a 1989 clinical review published in the journal "Progress in Neuro-Psychopharmacology and Biological Psychiatry". This study stated that folic acid deficiency is very common among patients with psychiatric disorders, and found that symptoms of bipolar disorder are much more intense in those with a folate deficiency.

In addition to the above benfits, folic acid can be very helpful for two reasons. One, it serves as a great way to try and stabilize your bodies natural functions without having to deal with the side effects of medicine. The avoidance of such side effects are one of the leading reasons to seek alternative treatments. Two, it is one of the more low risk treatments you can undergo when batting bipolar disorder. This ease and effectiveness, combined with such a low risk, makes folic acid a great supplement to take. It has also been linked to helping with the production of neurotransmitters. This helps brain function, which of course is also important in helping with problems such as mood swings.

Folic acid is also a natural combative to depression as well as depressive symptoms. If you are suffering from depression in conjunction with low levels of either serotonin or folate, this can be a very good way to help that. As a neurotransmitter synthesizer, folic acid stimulates the production of seratonin which, as previously explained, is a natural mood stimulant. As such, the effects brought on by folic acid help with stopping depression. You can also use folic acid with other types of medication, such as B12 or antidepressants. Folic acid has been shown to further the beneficial effects of these drugs. In fact, folic acid and vitamin B-12 can improve the treatment outcomes of people suffering from depression because these nutrients work together to increase levels of S-adenosylmethionine, a chemical that plays a role in the manufacturing of serotonin.

While folic acid is very strong in helping those with bipolar disorder, there are some known side effects. However, it is important to know that these side effects are most commonly affected and caused by high levels of folic acids. Taking it at lower levels, due to the inherent low risk that comes with folic acid, should not be cause for concern. If you do take high levels of folic acid, you can experience many internal problems, such as abdominal cramps, upset stomach, nausea and diarrhea. These high levels may also bring about rash, sleep disorders, irritability, confusion, behavior changes, skin reactions, seizures or excitability. Due to the length of this list, it is always good to check with your physician and let them know when you are planning to take folic acid. However, if your doses are kept low, you should be fine.

Sources: *Rakofsky et al., Depression and Anxiety. 2014; 31:379*

Lakhan et al., Nutrition Journal. 2008; 7:1

15. Homeopathy

Homeopathy, which is a natural law of healing used more traditionally in ancient or eastern medicinal practices, is the next alternative treatment that will be covered in this guide. Homeopathy works, at its base, much like how vaccines or other similar drugs work. That is, using the problem your are facing in order to overcome that problem. Vaccines take a part of a drug and put it into a person in order to help a person fight that disease. Homeopathy, while more of a mentality rather than a set practice, is built around a very similar type of thinking.

The golden rule in homeopathy is "likes are cured by likes". That is to say, you can only cure (or in this case help treat) something by using a part of the thing that is hurting you. Much like the above example, if you are suffering from something, using that thing can give you the most relief. Fighting fire with fire, if you will. In the case of bipolar disorder, this brand of homeopathy stems from tackling the biggest problems most commonly associated with the disorder; depression, anxiety and quality of life.

This is done by taking small doses of certain homeopathic medicines, which are supposed to help you overcome your illness. Here, the doses produce smaller effects of the problems, creating many similar symptoms of depression and anxiety. Then, through this, the patient will overcome the problem by learning how to properly fight it. While it is an unconventional way to deal with diseases, homeopathy has been found to be very effective at helping many different diseases, particularly bipolar disorder.

In a study, (*Qureshi et al., Neuropsychiatric Disease and Treatment. 2013; 9:639*) homeopathy and homeopathic effects were used to help people suffering from different mental health problems. After undergoing homeopathic treatment, almost all of the patients showed positive improvements in their mental health. An audit of UK homeopathic clinics revealed that more than 84% of consultees reported improvement in mental health problems (including depression) and improvement in well-being. None of the 273 patients in that study reported deterioration, and use of conventional medicines was reduced in 25% of patients. While it can be hard to determine the exact meaning of these results due to different kinds of homeopathy, these are still very positive improvements.

The two largest problems that homeopathy has helped solve, are complications associated with depression and anxiety. This is why this form of treatment has been deemed to be so beneficial to those with bipolar disorder. Bouts of depression are one of the most harmful effects to those with bipolar disorder, and anxiety is a large side effect of mania. In this way, while it does not help to necessarily stabilize moods, using homeopathy does help with problems that come from each side of the mood swing. The data for this showed positive outcomes were most frequently observed in irritable bowel syndrome (73.9%), depression (63.6%), and anxiety (61.0%). However, what caused the beneficial outcome for these treatments is quite unclear, and still needs more data to be fully conclusive. Still, in this same vein, due to the data that has already been collected, there have to be large-scale trials in order to prove that this method of homeopathy is in any way ineffective at helping with mood disorders.

Homeopathy, in addition to its physical benefits, has the added bonus of being a relatively safe alternative treatment. Homeopathic medicine, while mimicking more dangerous symptoms, is generally very safe. This even goes for higher dilutions, where other medicines would typically become unsafe. The main thing you want to be cognizant of when dealing with homeopathy is being as safe as possible. Due to this low-risk nature of the treatment, homeopathy can only go wrong if you do not take the proper precautions. Ineffective preparations are one example of this, but if you plan accordingly and understand how exactly homeopathy works, you should be fine. One additional indirect risk associated with this practice is replacing effective conditional therapies. You always want to make sure that normal, more proven therapies are not right for you (whether this is medicine or some other venue) before undergoing something such as homeopathy. However, if you do find that you want to try an alternative, this is a great avenue to take for both anxiety as well as depression.

Sources: *Qureshi et al., Neuropsychiatric Disease and Treatment. 2013; 9:639*

BIPOLAR DISORDER:
35 OUTSIDE OF THE BOX TIPS TO MANAGE BIPOLAR DISORDER

16. Inositol

This section will break away from some of the previous treatments, and get into how you can help treat bipolar disorder from a molecular level. Here, the way to do that is using a compound known as Inositol. This molecular compound is a precursor in the phosphatidyl-inositol signaling pathway. This means that the pathway is controlled by the compound, which in itself is a glucose isomer, and is affected by the signaling of many neurotransmitters. We have already covered the importance of neurotransmitters in relation to both the mental health as well as bipolar disorder, and that importance is also relevant here. This section will cover two different studies that were conducted on inositol's effects on bipolar disorder in order to portray how effective it can be when used as a treatment. Inositol is a natural chemical that appears in both plants and animals. However, it can also be produced synthetically, which allows it to be taken in a more controlled form.

The first study we will look at (*Rakofsky et al., Depression and Anxiety. 2014; 31:379*) was conducted in 2014, and studied a range of different ways to treat bipolar disorder. In the study, researchers found some benefits associated specifically with those treated through the use of Inositol. Here, 28 patients were used. All of these patients were suffering from severe depression episodes caused by bipolar disorder. Each patient was administered the compound over a four week period. Though this trial did not give overwhelming evidence supporting its use in treating every effect of bipolar disorder, it was found effective in helping curb the signs or side effects of depression.

When breaking down the data, it is clear that the effects of Inositol are quite effective. Numerically, more patients responded to inositol (50%) than placebo (30%). Of the six inositol responders, five maintained their response throughout a 24-week post treatment follow up period. Two of three patients in the inositol group experienced a reduction in baseline tremor, while neither of the two patients with hand tremors in the placebo group experienced a reduction in their tremor. As part of the Systematic Treatment Enhancement Program for Bipolar Disorder, 66 BD type I or II depressed patients in a major depressive episode were randomized to 16 weeks of open-label treatment with adjunctive lamotrigine, inositol, or risperidone. All patients had demonstrated poor response to 12 weeks of a standard or randomized care pathway, or they had a history of failure to respond to at least two antidepressants or an antidepressant plus mood stabilizer.

This study demonstrates Inositol's potential to improve depressive symptoms over time. Most of the studies conducted of Inositol's effects on bipolar disorder came out negative, meaning that they showed positive effects. In this study, the data revealed significant effects of Inositol in helping people fight against depression and depressive states.

When looking at a second study (*Qureshi et al., Neuropsychiatric Disease and Treatment. 2013; 9:639*) the positive benefits of Inositol become even more clear. Here, Inositol was found to be much more effective than a placebo, which is another indicator of its benefits. This was particularly relevant in treating both depression and panic disorder. At first, when a randomized control trial was conducted on 24 bipolar patients given inositol or a placebo, no significant differences between the treatment groups was found. Still, the studies were conducted again using larger groups to increase the sample size. Another study of 66 bipolar I or II patients with resistant depression examined the benefits of augmenting mood stabilizers with lamotrigine, inositol, or risperidone. They discovered that the rate of recovery was 23.8% with lamotrigine, 17.4% with inositol, and 4.6% with risperidone. This boost furthers the claim that inositol is an effective treatment. This second trial, with the larger sample size, is one of the reasons scientists found it to be so effective. When taking inositol, it is best to take it in dosage based on how much you need. This can range from anywhere between 12,000 to 20,000 mg/day.

In the above treatments, Inositol was given with other types of medicine, such as mood stabilizer and lithium. A combination of this compound with the other medicines was were it was the most effective, and gave the best results. When taking inositol, increased flatulence can occur. In a more serious side effect, is has also been found to increase bouts of mania in isolated cases. However, these bouts of mania brought on by using inositol are few and far between, making it much less of a worry.

Sources: *Rakofsky et al., Depression and Anxiety. 2014; 31:379;*

Qureshi et al., Neuropsychiatric Disease and Treatment. 2013; 9:639

17. Light Therapy

As a direct contrast to the method of dark therapy, here we will look at using light therapy to treat bipolar disorder. As you can imagine, light therapy is exactly what it sounds like, using light or exposure to light to help with bipolar disorder. Exposure to light has been found to have many powerful benefits, and light therapy is a good way to help people cope with mental disorders. This can bring a lot of different positive results, and can be a very good treatment to those suffering from the effects of bipolar disorder.

Light therapy was first developed to treat a mental illness known as seasonal affective disorder, or SAD. SAD causes depression in people who are immersed in a dark environment for too long. Here, light is used as a way to cheer them up, and offset the depression they are feeling. Artificial light has been used as an effective way to treat SAD for quite some time. When treating SAD, artificial light serves as a way to help people who fall into a funk during the winter time. However, more and more applications of artificial light in treating different ailments have been coming to the forefront in the past years. Of these are applications for treating bipolar disorder. This mainly stems with artificial lights natural ability to help with depression. Light therapy has also been linked to helping those who have suffered from brain injury.

Light therapy is also known as "bright light therapy" or "phototherapy". During the treatment process, bright, artificial light is administered to the patient through the use of a light box. This box contains fluorescent bulbs as well as a diffusing screen. Once the patient is ready to begin, they are exposed to the light. While it is not recommended that you look directly into the light when undergoing phototherapy, the patient should be turned towards the light source. This exposure is what usually garners the best mental results of using this form of therapy. The light intensity in this process usually sits somewhere between 2,500 and 10,000 lux.

Another benefit of light therapy is how quickly it works. Many drugs and treatments can take some time to kick in so it is beneficial to get one that works quickly. Onset of therapeutic effect commonly occurs somewhere between 3 and 7 days after the treatment is administered. This quick turn around time is one of the best reasons to use this therapy beyond its proven effectiveness.

There are many kinds of light, and in order to ensure phototherapy works best for the individual patient, there are four specific elements that make up phototherapy. The first of these elements is intensity, by which one controls how bright the light they are being exposed to is. Commonly, this is between 5,000 and 10,000 flx. The next element of phototherapy is the wavelength of the bright-light device. This device can vary greatly, but uses the entire spectrum of visible light when being used for therapy. It should be noted that a personal head lamp can also be used as a way to administer light to a patient, but this is generally not recommended.

When undergoing light therapy, patients want to be aware of the next part of phototherapy, distance from light. Just as you do not want to stare directly into the light, it is also advised that those undergoing this style of therapy should be a safe distance away from it as well. Researchers recommend that this distance should be 60 to 80 centimeters away from the light source. Another important part of phototherapy is the duration of the procedure itself. It is found that in most patients, light therapy has been to shown to be much more effective in the morning. There are isolated incidents of the evening being more effective for some people, but overall, morning is the ideal time to undergo this treatment.

Though data is scarce on the effects of phototherapy, it has shown great promise in the past few years to helping those with bipolar disorder. On its own, just as in the case of seasonal affective disorder, light therapy can help fight depression. If you want to use phototherapy, using it with other antidepressant medication can further its effects towards helping you with depression. Light therapy is hypothesized to benefit by a variety of mechanisms. One such suggested mechanism is by light-induced suppression of melatonin secretion by the pineal gland. Another proposed mechanism of benefit is by correcting the circadian rhythm. As a method, it can also lead to a better, more sound sleep. All of these reasons are why light therapy can be a great addition to your normal medication or therapy regimes.

When using a lightbox as a way to treat your symptoms, always do so while supervised. Supervision or help can be very important to this procedure, as some prolonged cases have shown a risk of increased mania. Beyond that, the number of side effects for this method are pretty standard with constantly being close to bright lights. Headaches are common to those undergoing light therapy, as are eye strain. Sleep disturbances can happen and, as already covered, there can be an increase in mania (in which case this treatment may not be for you). Agitation and mood instability can also occur, and you should always be under supervision when using light therapy as a method of treatment.

Sources: *Pail et al., Neuropsychobiology. 2011; 64:152*

Agargun et al., Chronophysiology and Therapy. 2013; 3:53

Parry et al., Dialogues in Clinical Neuroscience. 2003; 5:353

18. Magnesium

Lithium, or lithium carbonate, is one of the most popular medications used to treat bipolar disorder. In this section, while we will not be covering lithium, but we will be covering a very similar drug: magnesium. Magnesium is a natural ingredient that can be taken as a supplement. In this, the way it is used as well as the way you can get it, are very similar to folic acid. Taking magnesium can have some health benefits, and can also act as a good way to increase sleep among other benefits.

Some patients undergoing bipolar disorder have been found to have magnesium deficiencies. This can be problematic, as magnesium is one of the main ingredients needed for nerve and muscle regulation. However, as it is produced in pill form, it is very easy to take magnesium if you are suffering from a deficiency. Magnesium is also found in different elements of nature. Whole grains and dark, leafy vegetables have high amounts of magnesium. If you want to increase your magnesium levels without taking pills or supplements, it is recommended to add these to your diet.

A study in 2006 published in 'Medical Hypothesis' suggested that depression may be caused by damaged to neurons. This damage only occurs when there is a lack of magnesium in the system. As such, by replacing magnesium levels, this damage could be corrected, which in turn could help fix the depression. In this study, the effects of magnesium went beyond that. Researchers found that the compound also helped with symptoms of irritability, insomnia, as well as anxiety. All of these are symptoms of bipolar disorder, which reveals how using magnesium goes beyond simply decreasing levels of depression.

One of the most alarming effects of both bipolar disorder and depression, is suicide. Suicidal thoughts can happen during periods of depression in bipolar patients. Magnesium can help with this, as seen in a study published in the February 1985 issue of "Biological Psychiatry" which linked high suicide levels with low levels of magnesium. Suicide attempts were seen much more commonly in patients who had low magnesium levels than those who did not. This was found across all disorders where people suffered from depression, but was especially true of patients with bipolar disorder.

Magnesium has also been found to help with many effects of mania as well as overall mania. Increased talking, inflated self-esteem, decreased need for sleep, racing thoughts and increased activity were all found to be minimized by using magnesium sulphate as a way to mitigate them from happening. This was found to be effective most commonly in patients who had been resistant to other common treatments, such as lithium and clonazepam. Magnesium can also be a very good choice instead of lithium. This is due to the fact that magnesium is very similar to lithium and, while it still had side effects, its side effects are not quite as severe. As a result, it is seen as a safer alternative.

Furthering out look at the benefits of using magnesium it has also been found to increase sleep in those with bipolar disorder, which helps set the all important light-dark cycle. Not only that, but magnesium leads to more sound, peaceful sleep as well. Magnesium, in conjunction with calming down mania, has also been linked to helping curb rapid cycling. In this way, it acts as a form of mood stabilizer, and can work as a way to have calming effects on the body.

As it operates very similarly to lithium, magnesium supplements do come with their share of side effects. These side effects can be more severe than most of what we have covered, but, as aforementioned, these are commonly not as extreme as lithium. These symptoms are centered around the digestive system, such as nausea and intense bouts of vomiting. Upset stomach can also occur, as can diarrhea. These may be uncomfortable, but are much better than the problems that magnesium is treating.

There are many positive effects to taking magnesium, and it is especially helpful to those who either have hard times with lithium, or who find magnesium to be ineffective as a form of treatment. If you are suffering from depression, anxiety, insomnia, or many other common problems associated with bipolar disorder, it may be a good idea to try and use magnesium. Remember, before trying supplements, you can always try to increase magnesium levels in your diet. This may allow you to get the amount you need without suffering any of the side effects. However, this only goes when using this in combination with other medicine. If you want to switch from lithium to magnesium, you need to take the recommended supplements.

19. Massage Therapy

When discussing exercise we covered how important a strong, healthy body can be when working on building a healthy mind. We will reference the link between body and mind here to bring up another form of therapy: massage therapy. The benefits of massages on both physical and mental health have been cited many, many times throughout modern medicine. As such, using it as a way to help with bipolar disorder is not a stretch by any means. In this section, we will look at a study to go over how effective massage therapy can be, and why it works so well as a form of treatment.

Massage therapy is, as its name implies, a form of therapy that acts very similar to a conventional massage. This treatment uses work with a trained professional in order to get heal your body. This is done through muscle manipulation, as well as applying pressure to certain muscles. This creates a relaxed state, and can be very beneficial to your body. Then, as a result, you also get a sounder, healthier mind state as well. These improvements can do some great things towards helping with many common effects that come with bipolar disorder.

Currently, there is no conclusive evidence supporting the use of massage therapy in the specific of treatment bipolar disorder. However, as is the case with multiple treatments in this guide, this method has been proven to help with the effects of bipolar disorder. In this case, while massage therapy is not distinctly a treatment for bipolar disorder in the traditional sense, it has been shown to improve symptoms of depression, which is one of the most common causes people with bipolar disorder exhibit. In fact, the effects of massage therapy helping with overall depression have been cited in a journal (*Andreescu et al., Journal of Affective Disorders. 2008; 110:16*) which we will reference here.

There are a couple of different types of massage therapy, all of which have proven to have benefits in relation to lasting depression.

Aromatherapy massage, which combines the sense of smell with traditional massage therapy, has been shown to help with mild forms of depression as well as anxiety. If you are seeing problems with sleep disturbances in conjunction with depression from bipolar disorder, you might want to try foot reflexology massage therapy; a method which has been shown to help with those problems. When treating depression, massage therapy has been found to help pregnant women, patients with HIV, and patients suffering from end-stage renal disease. While none of these examples are directly related to those who are living with bipolar disorder, this range does show just how good massage therapy can be when treating depression.

While there is much debate as to why massage therapy is so effective in helping treat depression, it may be due to the higher levels of cortisol level. In addition, this treatment has also been seen to increase levels of serotonin and dopamine which, as already covered, is one of the best ways to combat depression. When looking at adolescents, attenuation of frontal EEG asymmetry in depressed patients was also reported with both massage therapy and music therapy. Additionally, yoga, which can fall into the realm of massage therapy, may also yield benefits in dealing with depression.

To further explain the effect of this treatment, we will quickly look at the results of five randomized controlled trials were systematically reviewed in 2004. All five trials reported positive findings, and each one gave credence to using massage therapy as a method toward combating depression. However, it should be noted that the variability in designs and methods (each trial utilized a different form of yoga and the severity of depression ranged from mild to severe) warrants a cautious interpretation of these results One of these five studies compared the relative antidepressant efficacy of electroconvulsive therapy, imipramine, and yoga in patients with melancholic depression and it reported remission rates of 93%, 73%, and 67% respectively

Massages, due to their therapeutic nature on both mind and body, also decrease levels of stress. Stress is a very common form of distress, much like depression and anxiety, that is very important for bipolar patients to combat. By reducing stress, it can cut down on many mental problems by putting your mind in a much better state. Massage therapy causes a reduction of stress through both a lowering of stress hormone levels as well as increase in both serotonin and dopamine production.

The side effects that come with massage therapy are relatively minor when compared to other treatments used to help bipolar disorder. Soreness is generally the only adverse effect of the method. However, some internal injury may happen in isolated cases. Allergic reaction to the oils can also occur, but this can easily be fixed by checking to see if any of them contain chemicals that are bad for you.

Soucres: *Andreescu et al., Journal of Affective Disorders. 2008; 110:16*

20. Meditation

We will now have take a break from looking at the body, and focus on treatments that help betterment through the mind. This section will cover a very old mental practice that has become more popular as of late, meditation. Meditation has many uses for different disorders, but can have some very pertinent implications for treating bipolar disorder. These holistic healing properties are some of the reasons that meditation is so helpful.

Meditation works in a very similar vein to other mental treatments in that it can be very effective in helping deal with bipolar disorder. There are several types of meditation, and each of them can help with the effects of bipolar disorder. These can range from the lotus position, where one sits in a cross-legged position (focuses on the physical aspect) in order to channel the best thoughts, to Samadhi, where one focuses on a certain idea or word. All of these combine the physical body with breathing practices, which combine to have beneficial effects on the body and mind. In recent years, there has been a growing interest within the medical community to study the physiological effects of meditation (*Venkatesh et al., 1997; Peng et al., 1999; Lazar et al., 2000; Carlson et.al, 2001*). The study of the positive aspects of medication on bipolar disorder are just one of these studies.

Meditation, at its base, is built around the idea of equalization. This even goes for moods, which are unbalanced in the case of those with bipolar disorder. When undergoing meditation, bipolar patients have found greater bouts of peace, and more stable moods for the hours after. Eventually, these effects permeate to other areas of your life, which in turn gives you a better mental state. This mental state makes patients much less prone to mood swings.

Another reason to the effectiveness of meditation is that the practice of meditation mimics many of the benefits from bipolar medications. As

73

the brain is the focus of those with bipolar disorder, most medications seek to deal with neurotransmitters production and stimulation. Insufficient serotonin, dopamine and GABA can all lead to adverse effects on overall mood and mental health. However, meditation acts to help stimulate these neurotransmitters much in the same way that traditional medicine does. As such, it has been shown to improve moods and give some relief to those with bipolar disorder.

As it acts with the physical form, meditation does have its share of effects on different physiological aspects as well. Of these, one of the most important is stimulating the brain's prefrontal cortex. The prefrontal cortex is a very important part of the mind that helps control logical thinking, such as knowing right from wrong, or good from bad. Meditation has been shown to stimulate this cortex, which in turn gives way to more set styles of thinking, something that can become difficult to those with bipolar disorder. This part of the brain has also been linked to certain personality disorders, the most common of which being depression. Meditation's ability to effect this part of the brain can boost this region, which can limit both periods of mania as well as depression.

Another large part to why meditation can be so good for those dealing with bipolar disorder is how it affects a person. Meditation can affect a person on two different levels. The first of these is the calm that comes from the actual practice. Meditation brings a relaxed state during the initial sessions, and this sense of calm can help normalize brain function when it comes to things such as anxiety, stress or mood swings. The second level of these stems from the accumulation of positive effects over time. That is, the results that last longer than the actual practice. While much of meditation is focused on bettering your body, much of it is also built on the mind. By changing your thoughts and general feeling to the world around you, it can give you a deeper sense of calm. This sense of calm that comes from this thinking is one of the best ways to combat depression. Meditation has even been found to induce a host of biochemical and physical changes in the body collectively referred to as the "relaxation response" (*Lazar et.al, 2003*). The relaxation response includes changes in metabolism, heart rate, respiration, blood pressure and brain chemistry. As such, meditation has the ability to strengthen all different parts of your body.

Self-reflection is a big portion of meditation. It is what the makes the process so effective, and allows you to see the world in a new way. However, this can also lead to some unwanted side effects as well. Paradoxical increases in tension and anxiety can occur to those who use meditation. It has also been found to, in some cases, trigger strong emotions and psychosis-like symptoms. Yet, using meditation is very positive, and can be a great way to put your mind at ease.

Sources: *Perich et al., Behavior Research and Therapy. 2013; 51:338*

Bipolar Disorder:
35 Outside of the Box Tips To Manage Bipolar Disorder

21. Mindfulness-based Cognitive Therapy

Mindfulness Based Cognitive Therapy (MBCT), which will be laid out in the following section, is another type of treatment that focuses almost completely on interactions in the brain. However, instead of trying to solve mental issues by way of special techniques, this process rather keeps its focus on the emotional side of the brain.

Mindfulness Based Cognitive Therapy is an idea of thinking that fuels treatment through changing your mindset in a very similar way that traditional meditation does. However, this type of thinking, rather than trying to understand your environment or project your ideas to greater themes, is centered around focusing in on the present moment. By focusing in on the current moment in a non-judgemental way, it allows you to better expand your style of thinking and help your current brain state. MBCT is not quite a form of meditation on its own, as can be inferred by the above sentences, but rather a type of thinking that can worked in with many other types of treatment. Commonly, when using MBCT to setback symptoms of bipolar disorder, those of which will be covered below, you want to combine it with other practices, such as group or cognitive therapy. This combination will allow you to garner the best results from this treatment as possible.

Mindfulness-based Cognitive Therapy was researched in a journal (*Qureshi et al., Neuropsychiatric Disease and Treatment. 2013; 9:639*) to better analyze why this type of therapy has been so effective as a form of treatment. According to the data, changing or altering a patient's mind can have very positive results that transfer to the physical form. These can have especially large effects on those who are living with bipolar disorder, as helping the mind is the most pertinent way to combat the disorder. A person suffering from bipolar disorder has many problems that all stem from the way their mind works, or the way their brain perceives the world. Allowing a new perspective can greatly help with those symptoms.

In the study cited above, mindfulness therapy practices were found to help greatly with depression. Additionally, it was also found to have effects of helping with anxiety and stress as well. In this way, MBCT is very good at reducing natural stresses that occur with bipolar disorder. Additionally, it has been found to play a major role in reducing negative effects while enhancing positive ones. For instance, this therapy has been used to decrease rumination as well as avoidance, but can also increase both feelings of acceptance and self-compassion. This process has also been found to help to attenuate non-relevant information processing.

MBCT, as it is a relatively non-invasive treatment focused solely on changing your mindset in response to the world around you, has no side effects. Most meditation practices, though some can cause problems with mania due to the shifting mind, are relatively harmless. This is one of the reasons they are seen as so effective when it comes to a form of alternative treatment. Not only are they good ways to get results without having to turn to more harmful methods, such as traditional medication, but they also have been shown to yield results while minimizing the amount of harm to your boy.

Due to the ease, safety and relative quickness of the treatment, MBCT is commonly used with those who are experiencing more serious signs of depression. These are commonly things such as suicidal thoughts or thoughts of self-harm. However, due to its effectiveness, it can also be used for any level of severity. If you are feeling distress due to bipolar disorder, this is a very good, risk free treatment to try. Especially if the medicine you are currently using is not giving you the desired effect, or if the side effects of that medication have proven to be too strong.

Sources: *Qureshi et al., Neuropsychiatric Disease and Treatment. 2013; 9:639*

22. Omega-3

Returning to the discussion on vitamins and other supplements, omega-3 fatty acids are a very important chemical compound that is commonly found to be scarce in those suffering from a wide range of mental disorders. Of course, this includes bipolar disorder, and this section will analyze how taking omega-3, or incorporating more of it into your diet, can have some very positive results and ramifications.

Like most supplements, omega-3 fatty acids naturally occur in many types of food. These acids are mostly found in seafood (commonly fish such as salmon and tuna) as well as green vegetables (asparagus, broccoli, greenbeans). As a result, simply increasing the amount of these foods in your diet is a good way to make sure you are getting the proper levels that you need. Another type of this acid, omega-6, which serves a very similar purpose, is found in many contrasting foods; such as animal fat, vegetable oil and margarine. Studies show (*Lakhan et al., Nutrition Journal. 2008; 7:1; Andreescu et al., Journal of Affective Disorders. 2008; 110:16*) that a large ratio imbalance of omega-6 to omega-3 is a linking factor between those with different mental disorders. In fact, a high dietary ratio of omega-6 to omega-3 has been suggested to lead to vulnerability to various physical and mental illnesses. Low fish consumption, in addition with low intake of fruits and vegetables, has been linked to many communities with high rates of mental disorders.

If you do have an omega-3 or omega-6 deficiency, it is often a good idea to take supplements of the acid in order to help offset these low levels. The best way to do this is by a dosage of 500-1000 milligrams/day. This will give you the proper amount you need while also not causing you to intake too much. One to two grams of omega-3 fatty acids taken daily is the generally accepted dose for healthy individuals, but for patients with mental disorders, up to 9.6 g has been shown to be safe and efficacious. In addition, numerous clinical trials, including doubleblind and placebo controlled studies have been run on this subject. These studies have shown that 1 to 2 grams of omega-3 fatty acids in the form of EPA added to one's daily intake decreases manic and depressive symptoms better than placebo. This gives ample evidence to the effectiveness of omega-3 acids in helping with symptoms of bipolar disorder.

Low levels of omega-3 have been linked to both depression and anxiety, which is one of the best reasons to make sure you are at a constantly high level of the fatty acids. Incorporating omega-3's into your diet, along with taking supplements of the acid, are both effective ways to make sure this does not happen, which in turn reduces your levels of distress. Lower distress levels then lead to lower levels of mood swings, which elevated the overall quality of life.

Omega-3 fatty acids have numerous other benefits in addition to the ones we have already covered. Another of these benefits is they can moderate neurotransmitter metabolism and alter neuronal membrane fluidity. Both processes can be very important as they augment bipolar depression and cardioprotective effects. However, if a patient is on anti-coagulants due to bleeding tendencies, it is often recommended that taking doses of omega-3's should be monitored.

Studies have also shown that these oils can be helpful because cells within the brain require them for signal tranmission. In this same vein, they are also a necessary part of proper, rational thinking, moods and also emotions. Omega-3's effect on these functions may be one of the causes as to why such low levels can lead to a higher probability of developing mental disorders.

When taking omega-3's beyond your normal diet, you do want to exercise a certain level of caution. However, you should be fine as long as you keep your intake to a normal level. Numerous studies have shown that up 2 grams of EPA (omega-3 fatty acid) taken daily is sufficient for decreasing symptoms of several mental health disorders with no side effects. When side effects from Omega acids do occur, it very commonly nausea related. There is a slight risk of hypomania, and bleeding episodes due to reduction in platelet aggregation as well. Some may even experience a fishy after taste. Being responsible, and sticking to a set amount of dosage, should prevent these symptoms from ever developing into a serious problem. If any do develop into something more than mild irritation, it is best to contact your doctor. Still, omega-3 fatty acids can be a great way to try and deal with distress that comes with both anxiety and depression. Many treatments in this guide focus on curbing depression, one of the most serious side effects of bipolar disorder, and omega-3's are no exception.

Sources: Lakhan et al., Nutrition Journal. 2008; 7:1; Andreescu et al., Journal of Affective Disorders. 2008; 110:16

BIPOLAR DISORDER:

35 OUTSIDE OF THE BOX TIPS TO MANAGE BIPOLAR DISORDER

23. FEWP and other Herbs

In addition to the dosing of supplements, there are many alternative, herbal options that will allow you to curb your symptoms. These work in a very similar vein to medication, However, herbal alternatives to traditional medicine is a popular choice for several reasons. One, they can provide desired effects when medicine is found to not beneficial (something that can happen to those with bipolar disorder). Two, herbal treatments tend to be less harmful to the body than medication, and are commonly found to have less side effects. Here, we are going to cover a couple of specific herbal treatments to study and understand the way they come together to work as a treatment.

The focus of this section will be on a method called Free and Easy Wanderer Plus, or FEWP. This acronym, FEWP, is a Chinese herbal compound which is thought to have antidepressant and anxiety relieving properties. As such, it can be seen to have positive effects on those battling with bipolar disorder. Not only is FEWP very beneficial as a treatment, but so if saffron, another herb that cures similar symptoms. To understand how effective each of these can be, we will look at a couple of different trials which give these methods some validity.

In a study (*Qureshi et al., Neuropsychiatric Disease and Treatment. 2013; 9:639*) a number of different herbs (saffron, lavender, Echium, and Rhodiola rosea) were found to show good results in mild-to-moderate depression when used alone or in combination with antidepressants. This reveals how herbal medication can be used as either a replacement or complement for more traditional medicines. In a similar study, researchers reported positive results of the aforementioned herbs in mild-to-moderate depression, anxiety, and sleep disorders. In a clinical trial of Free and Easy Wanderer Plus (FEWP, Golden Flower, People's Republic of China; a Chinese herbal extract formula, fluoxetine, and placebo) 150 patients with post-stroke depression showed significant improvement with both FEWP and fluoxetine compared with placebo. At the end of the trial, subjects on FEWP showed greater improvement than those traditional medicine. This study suggests that FEWP can be used safely with few side effects in patients with post-stroke depression. While not pertaining specifically to the treatment of bipolar disorder, this does give credence to how effective this mix of herbs can be.

All 11 parts of the FEWP compound have been tested (*Ravindran et al., Journal of Affective Disorders. 2013; 150:707*) time and time again to show how effective it is in dealing with both unipolar as well as bipolar depression. FEWP has also shown significant Level 2 evidence of benefit as augmentation agent in bipolar depression. However, it is commonly recommended to only serve as a third-line adjunctive treatment. This is due to limited clinical experience outside of China, the country where it originated.

FEWP and herbal treatments can also work very well when combined with other types of medicine. For instance, when used as adjunctive treatment with carbamazepine, FEWP improved tolerability and decreased the risk of discontinuation. However, FEWP is also not the only combination of herbs that can help reduce stress to those with bipolar disorder. Other herbs, such as saffron and lavender, also showed effects in mild to moderate depression. This change was shown whether the patients used these supplements alone or with other types of medicine.

Despite the positive success rate, caution is always important when using herbs and dietary supplements. When nine plant species used for the preparation of herb in India, it was found they had heavy metal content that went beyond the World Health Organization limitations. Furthermore, heavy metals and organochlorine pesticides have been found in some dietary supplements in the United States. Cases of heavy metal poisoning have also been found in traditional Chinese medicine as reported by several investigators. As such, sticking to safe levels of dosing, while also making sure you are getting the correct mix of herbs, can reduce this risk of injury or adverse effects. Other side effects from herbal treatments that you should be aware of are headache, dizziness, diahrrea, constipation, dry mouth and tachycardia.

Herbal remedies can be very important to helping treat the or mitigate symptoms with bipolar disorder. FEWP can also be very strong when it comes to more traditional forms of depression or anxiety. However, beyond that, there are many different kinds of herbs, and they each have their own benefits and risks. As always, remember to do your own research. This will help you try the herbal treatments you want safely, and lead you to exactly what kind will work best for the specific symptoms you are experiencing.

Sources: *Ravindran et al., Journal of Affective Disorders. 2013; 150:707*
Zhang et al., Journal of Psychiatric Rsearch. 2007; 41:828
Qureshi et al., Neuropsychiatric Disease and Treatment. 2013; 9:639

24. Prodromal Detection Therapy

This section will focus on prodromal detection therapy, which is not so much a treatment as it is a way to making sure to stay as strong as possible. Bipolar disorder is a disease. As such, it can be thought of, studied and treated just like any other. Though health care officials are very good when it comes to monitoring your symptoms, and while medicine can also help with the reduction of problematic thinking, you are also a great resource for staying healthy. This mindset, teaching a patient how to effectively stay safe while living with bipolar disorder, is at the heart of prodromal detection therapy, and the theme that we will look at here.

To make sure prodromal therapy is effective, the patient must be taught about the signs to look for or be aware of in their everyday life. This will help prevent relapses into unhealthy bipolar behavior and can minimize destructive symptoms. In this, there is a long list of prodromal symptoms that patients are taught to watch out for. If these symptoms can be recognized, they can then be prevented. There are two types of prodromal symptoms to watch out for, and they differ based on either mania or depression. Examples of common prodromal symptoms for mania include: hostility, ideas of grandiosity, overreactivity, distractibility, uncooperativeness, reduced sleep, and ideas of persecution. Examples of the common prodromal symptoms for depression include: sadness, talking less, weariness, worrying, autonomic disturbance, indecision, reduced appetite, and difficulty concentrating.

Prodromes themselves are defined as the early signs and symptoms that herald a full-blown illness. Bipolar prodromes are any cognitive, behavioral and affective signs or symptoms that signal an oncoming episode. The prodromal period generally refers to the time interval between the onset of the first prodromal symptom and onset of the characteristic signs/symptoms of the fully developed illness. In this way, they are often very good indicators of a coming episode, and are often used as markers to keep such things straight.

Prodromal detection works through a system of prevention, which can be instrumental in stopping depression and mania. Medicine is often not enough to cause the prevention of relapses, and by raising awareness, prodromes detection most often does. The more aware one is about symptoms to watch out for, the better that can be prevented. In fact, early detection of prodromal symptoms can help delay relapses. As such, these can then be recognized, and there is usually enough time to get the necessary help. Using this technique, acute episodes can be prevented and adverse consequences avoided.

Another important role in podrome detection therapy is the role family members can play. As they are on the outside, it is found that family member can also detect symptoms, possibly even detecting them more than the patient themselves. In this way, when using prodrome detection, it is often very important to also include family members or those who interact with the patient often, as another line of defense against relapse.

In a study conducted to show how family members could perceive prodromes, seventy per cent of patients with mania reported prodromes prior to relapse. This was significantly less than the proportion of their relatives, ninety seven percent of whom reported prodromes in their loved one. This was also much lower than the proportion of patients with unipolar depression (93%), reporting prodromal symptoms among patients. The mean duration of the prodromal period reported by patients with mania was about 20 days, while relatives reported durations which were longer by about 5 days.

These results suggest that relatives appeared to be better at detecting prodromes than the patients with the disorder. This indicates the importance of involving a family member in any intervention program, and shows how it can helps with the detection of prodromal symptoms.

This can be a key strategy, and including relatives in this will not just make the process more efficient, but it will also improve the chances of the patient having a successful outcome.

This style of therapy, while important in helping those with bipolar disorder keep a happy, healthy life, has no real side effects. This is mainly due to the fact that is a mental practice. Medicine can be very helpful to those with bipolar disorder, but an active mind and awareness about certain symptoms can go a long way too. Bipolar disorder may not be treatable, but is can be prevented, and negative symptoms can worsen. Prodrome prevention therapy is one of the strongest ways to stop this from happening, and it may increase your quality of life.

25. Psychoeducation

In this section, we will cover a type of treatment that, much like podrome prevention therapy, works using a certain mindset in order to achieve a goal. Here, that mindset comes from a practice known as psychoeducation, which operats very similar to the above practice. However, unlike prodrome prevention, which focuses on raising awareness to make it easier for those to prevent relapse into bipolar symptoms, psychoeducation is more focused around thinking as a way to make sure patients have the most practical approach possible to helping with their disease. Though this, it also helps prevent patients from slipping into episodes of both mania and depression, but does so with a slightly different set of rules.

At its base, the goal of psychoeducation is to create prevention, and make the patient much better at coping with the symptoms that they have. Recognizing symptoms can bring amounts of both stress and anxiety, but if one properly prepares, these effects can be drastically lessened. In journalistic reports that we will go over in the following paragraphs, psychoeducation has been shown to have a multitude of benefits with no drawbacks. Of these, it has been show to improve adherence to treatment, which is very good at increasing quality of life. It also can improve illness management, which makes living with any disease, including bipolar disorder, much easier. Finally, psychoeducation works by teaching early recognition of recurrence in addition to coping strategies. This helps to prevent episodes as well as delays relapse occurrences related to the disorder.

One of the main points of psychoeducation is giving the patient a greater degree of control over the disorder. What that means is, it allows some level of allowance of the patient to collaborate with physicians on treating their disease. This gives them a larger sense of control over their disorder, and can raise positive thinking. Psychoeducation also blends a theoretical and practical approach to understanding and coping with the consequences of their illness, in the context of a medical model. The blending of all these styles is one of the main reasons that psychoeducation helps so much in preparing for bipolar disorder.

In a study (*Colom et al., Bipolar Disorders. 2004; 6:480*) conducted on looking at how psychoeducation can help those with bipolar disorder, researchers studied 120 people with bipolar disorder. In this, the group revealed the efficiency of psychoeducation in preventing all types of bipolar episodes and increasing time to relapse at 2-year follow up. The number of hospitalizations per patient was also lower for the psychoeducation group. To validate the results, this study was repeated once again, using a new set of patients. In the second study, which looked at patients with bipolar 1 disorder, the results were largely the same. This suggests that although psychoeducation is surely working through adherence enhancement, there may be other supplementary mechanisms of action. This include such things as early detection of prodromal signs and induction of regularity of habits, which are important components of the package. However, overall these show how effective psychoeducation can be.

Just as with prodrome prevention, psychoeducation has very little to no setbacks. This is largely due to the fact that is a prevention strategy rather than a set treatment. However, this does not diminish how beneficial such prevention strategies can be. In addition, having no side effects is what makes treatments such as psychoeducation so beneficial. Not only do they work great alongside other medicine, but they do not add any extra stress on your body and your health. Side effects of many treatments for bipolar disorder can be very difficult to deal with, and can have great effects on your body. Any type of treatment, prevention practice or method to treating bipolar disorder that has no side effects is always a welcome break. Psychoeducation is no exception to this rule, and because of this, should be a practice incorporated into many treatment plans.

In accordance to the above data and trials, psychoeducation has also been found to be particularly effective in combating suicidal thoughts or tendencies. In this same vein, psychoeducation has been seen as an effective way to treat particularly hard to treat patients as well. The results the above study also noted that early detection of prodromal signs in the trial were shown to be beneficial to preventing mania, but not signs of depression. However, psychoeducation, due to its thinking and state of mind, can be beneficial to any treatment. This is not a way to go on your own, but using prevention or psychoanalytic methods allows for patients to cope with bipolar disease in a way that they see fit. It can be very difficult to have a disease control your life, and methods such as this flip that, bringing about a much higher quality of life than they normally would have.

Sources: *Colom et al., Bipolar Disorders. 2004; 6:480*

BIPOLAR DISORDER:
35 OUTSIDE OF THE BOX TIPS TO MANAGE BIPOLAR DISORDER

26. Reflexology

Although we have already discussed the benefits of using massage therapy before, and while the following section does deal with a treatment very similar to massage, reflexology is a little different. While massage therapy hopes to heal and treat the mind using the relaxation of the body, reflexology actually targets certain spots of the body to conduce the healing process. This can have a wide range of benefits to the overall health, mind and body, on those with bipolar disorder, and even has several other uses as well. Here, we will cover the way this method works, why reflexology is such a good form of alternative treatment, and the different ways it can be applied to helping those with bipolar disorder.

Reflexology is a treatment that is built around applying pressure to certain parts of the body in order to generate healing properties. These areas are commonly the hands, feet, and ears. When doing this practice, the therapist will commonly apply pressure to certain spots in these areas, which can help restore energy balance. This method of applying pressure can also detect energy imbalances. Energy differences are usually related to imbalances in either the mind or your physical body. Restoring these imbalances is very important to reflexology, and can have a huge impact on how you live your day to day life.

Reflexology has a long list of positive benefits, most of which have great impacts on issues related to bipolar disorder. Relaxation, just as with massages, is the prime effect of reflexology. These pressure points create a sense of relaxation in your body, which can then translate to your brain. As such, this method is also beneficial for reducing stress and keeping as calm as possible. Energy can also be increased for those who undergo reflexology, which can be very good to those who are feeling side effects from medication or are under symptoms of depression. There are also many mental benefits to this treatment. Reflexology has been known to increase a sense of control, as well as feelings of happiness.

Beyond the above benefits, reflexology is also used as a natural way to induce sleep. We have covered in-depth how detrimental, and how common, a lack of sleep can be to those with bipolar disorder. Getting your necessary circadian rhythms is very important, as is making sure you sleep as soundly as possible. Reflexology, in accordance with its relaxing properties, enables a very good night's sleep. In addition, it also is very helpful in that is creates a much deeper sleep. This deep sleep will allow you to have many less sleep disturbances in addition to being able to sleep longer when using reflexology. The positive effects of this method of treatment also extend to a reduction in anxiety as well as depression. As a result of the above way the treatment can help, those with bipolar disorder have shown positive results when undergoing this as a form of therapy. Reflexology has also been revealed in different trials (*Andreescu et al., Journal of Affective Disorders. 2008; 110:16*) that it has many similar properties to massage therapy.

When undergoing reflexology, due to stress and pressure on certain parts of your body, there are some very important aspects of the treatment you should be aware of. The first of these is a process called "healing crises". These "crises" are simply the body's reaction to the treatment, but they can seem alarming if you are not aware that they exist. These crises often refer to adverse reaction to reflexology when the treatment is first started. Here, patients may experience many unpleasant side effects, such as nausea or fainting. However, this usually only lasts a couple of days or the first week, making it a pretty easy thing to overcome. Furthermore, these reactions are usually a good sign. Although that may seem strange, it is because they show that the treatment is actually working. Healing crises are usually signs that the body is dealing with toxins or poisons that build up when the treatment begins. As reflexology progresses, your body begins to excrete these damaging poisons. During this excretion is when the crises occur, and are merely a measure of the body attempting to clean itself.

The exact type of side effects you get from reflexology depends on what type of healing crises you experience (if at all). If you a experience one that affects the digestive tract, diarrhea, flatulence, vomiting and nausea are all common results. There is also the option of skin rashes or increased urination with stronger smelling or darker urine. If you have pre-existing arthritic pain, this might flare up. When undergoing the process of reflexology it is also very important to drink plenty of water. This is because, keeping your system well-hydrated and well-flushed will enable your body to better facilitate the detoxification process. The more liquid you drink, the quicker those toxins will leave your system. As stated, not everyone will experience a healing crisis, and most of the ones that are experienced will be relatively short, but you should be able to prepare for one should it arise.

Sources: *Andreescu et al., Journal of Affective Disorders. 2008; 110:16*

27. Reiki

On the path of restoring the body's energy and keeping levels at the right place, Reiki is another treatment that focuses on the mental much more than the physical for helping with many symptoms commonly associated with bipolar disorder. Reiki channels energy through the use of a meditative state between a practitioner and a patient. This process, as most energy based treatments are, revolves around reducing general distress. It can also bring about levels of relaxation, and is a good alternative for those looking to reduce distress through alternative means.

Reiki, or Reiki healing, is a natural healing process. As such, it also has very little to no side effects, which deems it one of the safer ways to help combat bipolar disorder. Reiki healing works by channeling vibrations through a person's body. When the vibrations within a person go up during the natural healing, negative energies are released. These negative energies are blockages that have been known to harm the body and can lead to further complications. Toxins stored in the body are also released during this process, which also has many positive effects. The releasing of these toxins is a very important part of Reiki. After being released, the toxins then enter the bloodstream and travel to both the kidney and liver. When the toxins enter these organs, it is filtered out of the body by way of the body's detox system.

Much like massage therapy and reflexology the effects of Reiki for bipolar disorder are centered around a lowering of distress. Excluding such harmful toxins from the body have been known to reduce different harmful effects. These effects include anxiety, which is one problem that can be extremely problematic for those with bipolar disorder. Reiki has even been shown to have a part in reducing depression as well. This goes right after the treatment happens, and can continue for up to weeks afterwards. After these positive benefits wear off, you can then simply schedule another Reiki session.

While Reiki can have some very good impacts on the body, its main use is actually to reduce side effects from other medical treatments. As covered, many problems of bipolar disorder stem from harmful or very impactful side effects of prescribed medicine. Much of this medicine can cause a lot of damage to the body, or make your life more uncomfortable than it has to be. By using Reiki treatment, these side effects can be reduced or even eliminated. Even if you are not experiencing large bouts of distress, it can often be a very good idea to try and use Reiki as a way to mitigate some unpleasant effects from other medications you are taking. This method has also been found to increase the natural state of healing as well, which can also be quite beneficial.

However, despite the fact that it is considered a relatively safe treatment, Reiki is not without its share of side effects. As Reiki works, the body begins to change. This change happens very rapidly, which can have some quick effects of the body. It is common for a person to feel some sort of weakness in their body as a result of these changes, which usually follows right after the healing session. Though, these symptoms may differ from person to person. Where one person may experience weakness or fatigue due to Reiki, others might feel a headache or perhaps discomfort in the stomach. Each person will respond to Reiki in a different way, and not all people will have side effects from the treatment.

A good way to stop negative side effects that can come from Reiki is to know the proper ways to respond to the treatment. Many of those who perform Reiki rest after healing. This will allow the body to properly recover from any effects that occur. In addition, just as with reflexology, it is always a good idea to try and drink a lot of water. Water is the best way to keep your body cleansed, and the best way to rinse out unwanted toxins. Staying hydrated is always key for recovery from such practices. Many also suggest it is best to not eat heavy meal after Reiki healing as they can cause some problems. However, as stated, a little bit of stomach discomfort can be a good sign. Other side effects of this healing are sleepiness, headache, and gastrointestinal complaints.

Sources: *Qureshi et al., Neuropsychiatric Disease and Treatment. 2013; 9:639*

28. Rhodiola

While many treatments in this guide have been beneficial in that they have all had a wide range of uses, this section will focus on one type of problem: depression. Here, we will take a look at Rhodiola, an herb that is also known as Rhodiola rosea. This is a supplement that can be a very good, all-natural way to help with depression or depressive symptoms.

Before we begin to discuss some of the findings between Rhodiola rosea and the symptoms of bipolar disorder, it should be noted that this plant has not been approved by the Food and Drug Administration (FDA) to prevent or cure any disease. However, that being said, trials have shown it to be very effective as a way to help with depression, which is what this particular section will focus on. Rhodiola rosea is a supplement that has been tested in various trials (*Qureshi et al., Neuropsychiatric Disease and Treatment. 2013; 9:639*), and these will be explained below.

When taking Rhodiola rosea extract, it is best to always follow the recommended doses. While these doses can vary based on your symptoms as well as what your body can handle, it was used at a set amount during a trial in Sweden (*SHR-5, Swedish Herbal Institute, Sweden*). This dose amount was 340 and 680 milligrams a day over the course of a six week period. While normally there are some mild side effects that can occur with Rhodiola, which will also be covered below, in this specific study, no adverse effects were seen or recorded. This is very good news, as it shows that, not only are the side effects of this supplement are mild, but they are also not seen in some patients.

The use of herbs such as Rhodiola have been used since ancient times. These are most commonly a practice of eastern medicine in today's world, however the uses of this have bled in the western world more as of late. In a recent university student survey that looked at the interaction between herb users and their medication (*Qureshi et al., Neuropsychiatric*

Disease and Treatment. 2013; 9:639) it was found that most herb use was self-prescribed (60%) and undisclosed to health providers (75%). Additionally, 34% of users took herbs to treat a mood disorder, 13% of herb users were taking concurrent prescription medication, and those who took both herbs and prescription medications had higher depression and anxiety scores than other herb users. However, more studies must be done in order to truly examine these interaction. Still, this data is provided for reference on herbal use and its effects.

Rhodiola is a supplement that has been prescribed for many different health problems, such as irregular menopause. However, the effect it has on depression, both mild and moderate, makes it very good for those who are experiencing the lows of bipolar disorder. Other studies, in addition to the ones above, has also proven to the antidepressant effects of Rhodiola rosea in use of treating certain mental disorders. While not clinically proven, Rhodiola rosea has been shown to be a mechanism of action in major depression is thought to be via beta-endorphins, tryptophan, and serotonin in the brain. All of these are seen as relatively positive effects, and all of them reduce depression.

Rhodiola, as can be seen by its properties to fight depression, is a mild stimulant. However, this can also cause some mild sleep problems. To avoid these sleep problems, it is suggested to take Rhodiola in the morning, as the stimulant effects should wear off by the night. Other possible side-effects that can come from this supplement are temporary vivid dreams and, in some cases, nausea. One other note is that women with a family history of estrogen-receptor positive breast cancer should be careful. This is because this herb binds the estrogen receptor. Beyond the assorted side effect, products containing 3% rosavins and 1% salidrosides were found to be effective in a randomized controlled trial. This means that they may be used to enhance the clinical effectiveness of Rhodiola rosea in fighting bipolar-related depression.

Sources: *Qureshi et al., Neuropsychiatric Disease and Treatment. 2013; 9:639*

29. S-adenosyl-L-methionine (SAMe)

This section will continue a discussion on the way supplements can help with bipolar disorder. This time, we will look at a compound known as S-adenosyl-L-methionine (or SAMe). SAMe is a natural derivative of the amino acid methionine and functions as a methyl donor in many different biological processes. Methionine is an amino acid that can be very helpful for different functions of the body. As such, SAMe can also be very helpful with certain parts. Just like with many of the compounds we have covered, patients with bipolar disorder have been found to have SAMe deficiencies. If you are experiencing such a deficiency, it is recommended to take 800 milligrams to offset it.

SAMe is a CAM (definition here please) product that has been tested under rigorous controlled conditions. This is beneficial in that it gives credence to the fact that this works very well as a treatment. SAMe has been investigated for its antidepressant properties in both open (*Lipinski et al.,1984*) and randomized controlled trials (*Mischoulon and Fava, 2002*). In these trials, SAMe was administered in doses of 200–1600 milligrams a day either orally or parenterally. Here, it was found to be much more effective than the placebo, always a must for any medication. The results from these studies were also effective as tricyclic antidepressants in alleviating depression, another good sign. However, when using SAMe some patients may require a higher dose to get the required effects. SAMe also may have a faster onset of action than conventional antidepressants, and may potentiate the effect of tricyclic antidepressants or of serotonin reuptake inhibitors. In this, oral dosages of SAMe up 1600 milligrams a day have also been found to bioavailable as well as safe (*Goren et al., 2004*).

The studies that have been done on the effects of SAMe have shown that is effective in decreasing depression. This is the main treatment that SAMe is used for, as no conclusive results have been found relating it to other forms of distress, such as anxiety or stress. The effects of SAMe have been proven in multiple studies to also potentiate the effects of SSRI's and tricyclic antidepressants. As a result, if you do suffer from depression, this is a very good treatment to use due to all of the available medical data, which may be scarce for other types of alternative treatments.

If you are planning to take SAMe as a way to combat any depression or signs of depression you may have, it is always a good idea to exercise caution. This is because, in bipolar patients, SAMe has been known to sometimes exaggerate some effects of mania or manic episodes. It can cause hypomania, or simply mania, and can have effect that lead to serotonin syndrome in patients who are using it while also on antidepressants. These adverse effects are not here to dissuade you from using SAMe, but rather as another example of the importance of being aware of what is going into your body. Proper research is a part of any medication, alternative or traditional, and it is always a good idea to try and explore the side effects or reactions before trying to take any new medication.

Continuing on the side effects, SAMe has also been associated with minor adverse effects, e.g., gastrointestinal symptoms and headaches (*Alpert et al., 2004*). These gastrointestinal symptoms include many internal discomforts such as nausea and diarrhea. Headaches can also occur when on SAMe, as can the switches to mania. Though there are many side effects that can occur, the studies showed that SAMe appears to be safe and efficacious in the treatment of depression. Further controlled studies may be needed to properly indicate this due to the fact that much of the current evidence comes from open trials or small controlled studies. More data is needed in particular to determine its effective dose and to better assess the risk of switch to mania or hypomania.

If you wish to use SAMe, it can be bought over the counter in most places around North America. While easily accessible, always check with your healthcare provider first before attempting to use it as a treatment. This goes double for SAMe due to its increased impact on those with bipolar disorder.

Sources: *Andreescu et al., Journal of Affective Disorders. 2008; 110:16*

Ravindran et al., Journal of Affective Disorders. 2013; 150:707

35 OUTSIDE OF THE BOX TIPS TO MANAGE BIPOLAR DISORDER

30. St. John's Wort

St John's Wort, the herbal therapy that will be the focus of this next section, is another natural way to treat depression. In this guide, we have already laid out many ways to treat depression, but remember, it is always important to choose one that works best for you. As cited in the introduction, the more types of treatment you are aware of, the more ways you can help yourself. Like other supplements, St. John's Wort is most often taken in a capsule. Here, St. John's Wort is one of the most used and oldest natural ways to treat depression. It has been around for thousands of years, and is currently one of the top selling herbs throughout the entire United States. In fact, in some countries, such as Germany, St. John's Worst has even had more prescriptions written for it that many prescription drugs (like Prozac). In fact, St. John's Wort, due to its properties and red sap, was even considered magical. While not magical, it is a great way to try to naturally deal with depression.

As aforementioned, St. John's wort is an herbal therapy that has been used for years to treat mild to moderate depression. We will look at a study (*Andreescu et al., Journal of Affective Disorders. 2008; 110:16*) in order to reveal validity behind that claim, and also study why exactly it can be such a good choice for those with bipolar disorder.

If you do decide you want to use St. John's wort, it is best to do so with a daily dosage between 500 and 1,100 milligrams. This will give you the desired effects you want, while not taking too much or too little. It should also be noted that this daily dose should be a standardized herbal extract that contains at least 0.3% hypericin for the desired effect.

Why St. John's wort works so well is relatively unknown. This is because the reasons behind the antidepressant properties are largely unclear. St. John's wort contains many different chemicals, which are called hypericin, pseudohypericin and hyperforin. Each of these chemicals have all been studied for antidepressant properties, but so far nothing has been found well enough to be concluded. However, the first studies on St. John's wort found that it served as a weak inhibitor of monoamine oxidase, or MAO. Another group of antidepressants (which include many monoamine oxidase inhibitors such as Marplan, Nardil and Parnate) work by this mechanism. This is important, because MAO is a substance that breaks down various neurotransmitters. The inhibition of MAO, which keeps it from breaking down control mood, includes such chemicals as dopamine, serotonin and noradrenaline. This allows these chemicals to stay working in the brain longer. When this happens, overall mood improves and generally stays higher longer.

Other research has shown that it may be due to the activation of adenosine receptors. The receptors are key in producing feelings of calmness. As such, by activating these sensors, it helps relax the patient. Malfunctioning GABA receptors, something else that this herb has been shown to help, can also cause depression and anxiety. By fixing these malfunctioning receptors, St. John's wort may help regulate mood. One more possibility of why this wort is so good as a antidepressant is through the activation of glutamate receptors. Disturbances at these receptors have been shown to lead to suicidal thoughts or extreme bout of depression. As with the above examples, fixing these receptors will fix the root of the problem as well.

This herb, when used as a treatment, is also beneficial in that it helps with serotonin production. Those with bipolar disorder who take St. John's herb will often have much higher levels of serotonin that those who do not, and this can be a huge boost in fixing the way that you feel.

For all of its positive benefits, St. John's wort has been linked to some side effects. Some of these are mild, while they can also scale to a much higher level. One of the side effects is the possible switch to mania, which can be triggered by this treatment. In addition, this has significant drug interactions. It has been shown to interfere with many prescription and nonprescription drugs. This is mainly due to the fact that St. John's wort can change how quickly the liver process drugs. If this happens, other prescription medication can leave the body faster than it should, which causes it to be much less effective. In addition, it can also directly interfere with the action of other drugs, either adding of subtracting from the other effects. For this reason, St. John's wort is often best used alone, or, if you are on medication, make sure it will not hinder what that is trying accomplish. More of the common side effects that are seen are photosensitivity, as well as seratonin syndrome. However, this syndrome only occurs when the wort is combined with SSRIs.

Sources: *Andreescu et al., Journal of Affective Disorders. 2008; 110:16*

31. Surgical Interventions:
Vagus nerve stimulation, stereotactic ablation, deep brain stimulation

Stepping away from herbal supplements and ways to heal the mind, surgical interventions are another tool that can be used to help with bipolar disorder. Surgical interventions are an array of different surgical practices and operations which can be very helpful in allowing you to live better with bipolar disorder. There is an assortment of different types of surgery that are available to treat mental disorders. However, in this section we will focus on three specific surgical interventions that all focus directly on symptoms of, or with, bipolar disorder. These practices are vagus nerve stimulation, deep brain stimulation and stereotactic ablation. Each of these practices have an array of benefits that can help lead you to a better life.

Vagus nerve stimulation is the first example of surgical intervention. Here, the vagus nerve, or the tenth cranial nerve, is stimulated by way of an electronic stimulator. This stimulator, once inside the patient, works by sending impulses to the left of the vagus nerve. These impulses are channeled through the body by a wire that sits just beneath the skin. This intervention was originally invented as a way to help combat epilepsy, but now has been used by doctors as a way to help with depression. The stimulating of this nerve causes a positive reaction in the brain that resists negative or harmful thoughts. A study done to record the results of this process (*Loo et al., Journal of Affective Disorders. 2011; 132:1*) showed how effective this treatment was.

In the study, analysis was gained using 25 patients with bipolar I or II diagnoses from a larger trial. Effects of vagus nerve stimulation, both short and long term (which refers to a time period of up to two years) were found to be similar in both bipolar and unipolar depression. When this study was expanded to include also a lack of manic symptoms, the response rate did not increase at all (*Nierenberg et al., 2008*). Another study, which was a pilot prospective, open-label study of nine rapid-cycling bipolar patients who were excluded from larger trials, was found to show benefits of this treatment over a 12 month period (*Marangell et al., 2008*).

The second surgical procedure, stereotactic ablation, works a little differently than vagus stimulation. Here, lesions are the way this process works to also cut down on depression. However, the depression that ablation helps is not the same as the depression in vagus stimulation. Vagus stimulation has been linked to helping medication-resistant depression, or depression that lingers on despite the use of medicine. In contrast, stereotactic ablation works to help resistant depression, which is depression that is typically hard to deal with. Because of this, many therapists try to employ this type of treatment in conjunction with their own help.

Stereotactic ablation, works when a professional makes lesions using either a thermal probe or radiosurgically. Due to the nature of this treatment, it is common that those undergoing ablation are typically drawn from the extreme end of the treatment-refractory spectrum. This is done, not only because of the treatment needed for such patients, but because it gives a good measure to compare outcomes across treatments. It is typically harder to achieve gains in subgroups undergoing ablation, which makes it harder to study. This method changes that. A recent prospective study followed 16 patients with otherwise intractable bipolar affective illness who underwent limbic leukotomy (subcaudate tractotomy and cingulotomy). At 7 years, mean depression severity declined over 50%, while BDI self-ratings declined 41%. Measures of anxiety and negative symptoms also declined. Two thirds of patients had a robust response on global measures.

The final type of surgical intervention is a process known as deep brain stimulation. This process is one of the most useful for those with refractory depression. Another implant is used here, this time to send pulses through a wire that specifically targets areas of the brain. In this way, it helps with depressive symptoms.

Now, this may not always be used, and even when it is implemented it is done so with caution. This is because, DBS has been found to trigger many adverse effect in bipolar patients, such as mania and hypomania. Because of this, going under deep brain stimulation can be risky for those with bipolar disorder. Yet, clinical observations from a single Bipolar I case do suggest that a combination of low-intensity DBS and multiple mood stabilizers might reduce induction of manic symptoms by DBS when treating bipolar depression (*B. Greenberg, unpublished observations*).

While each of these treatments have their own risk, they also have many benefits as well. Undergoing vagus nerve stimulation may have some adverse effects, such as risks from surgery. Pain or vocal cord paralysis may also occur. Following the surgery, there can even be hoarseness, breathing problems, chest pain, skin pain or difficulty swallowing. Thought we have already covered some of the side effects associated with deep brain stimulation, there are also some surgical risks associated with the treatment. These include things such as a risk of stroke or infection. Stereotactic ablation also has some side effects it is good to be aware of. These include risks for stereotactic ablation include edema, seizures, and personality changes. Surgical intervention may not be for everyone, but for those who are suffering greatly from bipolar disorder, or people who have tried many different treatments to no effect, these are reliable options.

Sources: *Loo et al., Journal of Affective Disorders. 2011; 132:1*

BIPOLAR DISORDER:
35 OUTSIDE OF THE BOX TIPS TO MANAGE BIPOLAR DISORDER

32. Tai Chi

Though surgical practices do come with their share of risks in helping the body through artificial means, the following section will cover a treatment that is rather the opposite. Tai chi is not only a natural way to help you with bipolar disorder, but it also creates that all important link between body and mind. Tai chi manages to create this through a building of both the physical and mental form. This strengthening is the core of tai chi, and is one of the sole reasons it has been found to be so beneficial in helping different disorders, bipolar disorder included.

Tai chi is an ancient practice that is a blend of both exercise, commonly lighter workouts and the relaxation that comes with meditation. To get a balance, the practice is an equal part of both meditation and exercise. Movements in tai chi, while helping the physical form, are typically carried out in a slower manner that allows you to better yourself. It also helps with breathing, which is one of the most important aspects of tai chi. Breathing is a great focal point for this treatment, as it incorporates each part of the body. Breathing has a natural calming effect, which is important for helping relax the mind. These things in combination have been shown to reduce a wide range of different problems, but the most important to this particular guide are symptoms of distress, particularly depression and anxiety.

For those with bipolar disorder, it is very important to make sure that you keep you distress levels are low as possible. This is because, such elements of distress can cause adverse symptoms that can lead to further complications. The best way to offset this is through things such as tai chi due its ability to relax both the body and mind. Tai chi is a subset of yoga, and acts as a form of yoga as well.

Tai chi was first invented by the Chinese as a form of self defense. However, that has been adapted in recent years to be used as a natural form of relaxation. In this way, it is used for both stress reduction as well as other health problems. It can also be applied to bipolar disorder, or any complications that arise as a result of bipolar disorder.

Tai chi was designed as a way to help promote serenity through its flowing and stretching movements. These are performed, just as with the breathing, in a very focused and slow manner. Typically, this deep breathing is accompanied by the movements. This allows you to find a sense of inner peace by relaxing your body. Although there are very few studies have been conducted to use tai chi specifically to bipolar disorder, there has been research which has routinely linked the practicing of tai chi with mood benefits.

Tai chi can be particularly beneficial to those with bipolar disorder who also belong to groups that tai chi is commonly recommended for. These groups are older adults as well as pregnant women. The reason that these groups use tai chi is due to its nature. Tai chi is a very low-impact exercise, which means that is helps the body in a healthy way while also reducing stress and natural pain that usually comes as a result of rigorous exercises. If you find that exercise helps with symptoms of your disorder, it may be good to try to use tai chi as your form of exercise to reduce any risks. This is especially true of older adults with more fragile bodies.

That is not to say that tai chi does not put strain on the body as well. Those who practice long periods of tai chi, or those who do it on a regular basis, can experience some of the more natural aches and pains that come with exercise. Soreness may be experienced, as well as some minor musculoskeletal aches and pains. However, these pains are commonly much lower than injury or pain that occurs with regular exercise.

In addition to helping with depression, tai chi has a range of miscellaneous benefits such as improved cognition, or stronger thinking. As we covered before in this guide, exercise is a valuable part of any wellness routine, and can be a very good practice that many people find they enjoy. However, exercises that also incorporate wellness practices, such as tai chi, often can be especially strong to those with mental disorders because of their impact on the mind.

33. Transcranial magnetic stimulation

For this next treatment, we will revisit the process of using electricity as a way to help brain function. Electricity, as explained in electroconvulsive therapy, can be beneficial when used in proper doses for treating bipolar disorder. This particular use of electricity is called transcranial magnetic stimulation (TMS), and uses both electricity and magnets to bring positive effects to the patient's brain. We will explore this method, which, although a little risky, has some great benefits when it comes to stabilizing the functions of the brain.

Transcranial magnetic stimulation works through an electromagnet. This magnet introduces a electric field to the brain, which helps both neuromodulation and neurostimulation. Each of these are important brain functions that the body needs to perform. In general, neuromodulation is very important because it is used for deeper circuits of the mind that go far beyond the cerebral cortex. As a result, it can have some very deep reaching effects. This is a contrast to the more conventional treatments of transcranial magnetic stimulation, which do not work as deep. Rather, these practices are focused on the outer neuron layers of the brain. Here, only the outer centimeter of the neural tissue is treated. However, despite this difference, each form of treatment has its own benefits. And, unlike other treatments that have been found to treat depression as a whole symptom, this method specifically treats the depression symptoms that come specifically with bipolar disorder.

In several studies and a few randomized trials (*Bersani et al., European Psychiatry. 2013; 28:30*) it was found that there was a moderate efficacy of standard TMS. As a result of the deeper magnetic field, which also showed less side effects, it usually expected that deep TMS can be more effective towards fighting bipolar disorder than standard TMS. To further expand upon this point, we will reference another study (*Harel et al.*), which is the leading literature on trials that study this interaction between TSM and the treatment of bipolar disorder.

This study looked at nineteen patients diagnosed as having bipolar disorder under treatment with psychotropic medication. Each of these patients received daily prefrontal deep TMS with H1-coil every weekday for four consecutive weeks; all pulses were delivered in trains of 20 Hz at 120% of the measured MT. Each of these sessions consisted of 42 trains with a 2 seconds duration for each. A 20 seconds intertrain interval (a total of 1680 magnetic pulses delivered per session) was also administered to them. The response was a 50% decrease of the Hamilton Depression Rating Scale (HDRS) score one week after the last treatment session. While this study does have some limitations, such as small samples of enrolled patients, concomitant medications, and lack of placebo simulations, the results clearly showed a higher efficacy of deep TMS than standard TMS for bipolar depression.

Deep transcranial magnetic stimulation is commonly used in conjunction with other treatments, which allows it to be much more effective. Adding it to other medications increases its effectiveness towards treating resistant bipolar episodes. In this way, it can be very good to anyone who is having a hard time overcoming their own problems. If these treatments continue, there is also a good chance that TMS will also help in maintaining euthymia. Euthymia is a term that refers to a generally positive or elated mood, something that can be hard to come by for some bipolar patients.

When undergoing transcranial magnetic stimulation, is it good to be aware of the potential side effects. This are usually mild, but do have a wide range. Scalp discomfort is one such problem that can occur, as are transient headaches. Furthermore, there can be many adverse effects, which may also include dizziness, insomnia, sensation of foul smell or bad taste, and generalize seizures. It is good to always be aware of how any treatment, regardless of what symptom it is for, is affecting your body.

Sources: *Bersani et al., European Psychiatry. 2013; 28:30*

34. Vitamins B, C and D

Vitamins B, C and D are three essential nutrients to any diet. However, they are connected to the treatment of bipolar disorder in that having proper levels of each of these is very important to a healthy body. Your personal health is extremely important, and we have already covered that a number of important vitamin deficiencies can be seen in those with bipolar disorder. Having low levels of these vitamins, even if not directly connected to bipolar disorder, can create problems that may worsen your health, which may worsen symptoms of the disorder.

Generally, if you are experiencing a deficiency of any of these essential vitamins, you are most likely going to need to take supplements in order to get your levels back to normal. While you can add some of these nutrients to your diet, as was the case with something such as magnesium, it will most likely not be enough to get your levels back to a set level. When using vitamin B6, it is best to take a dose of 100-200 milligrams a day. However, if you are experience low levels of B12, then you want to take 300 to 600 micrograms. For vitamin C deficiency, it is recommended to ingest one to three grams as a divided dose. These set amounts are important to follow, as taking too many vitamins can have some unwanted ramifications that will be covered later on.

Vitamin C, which is also known as ascorbic acid, is an extremely beneficial vitamin. It provides anti-inflammatory and antioxidant protection, while also increasing neurotransmitter synthesis. It also has many antioxidant effects. It has also been shown to fight depression, which is why fixing this imbalance can be important to those with bipolar disorder. For these reasons, vitamin C's positive attributes are quite important to the functioning of a healthy body and mind.

Though there have been many studies on how vitamin C can positively effect the human mind, the one specific study we will cite here (*Rakofsky et al., Depression and Anxiety. 2014; 31:379*) looked at its effects on those with bipolar disorder. In this, 24 bipolar patients took place in a two-day, cross-over, double-blind, placebo-controlled study. 12 of these patients suffered from depression. During the process, patients were rated hourly on a global illness scale and twice on the Hamilton Rating Depression Scale (HRDS). The global illness scale rating of the depressed patients on vitamin C was significantly lower than those on the placebo. This went for 3,4,5 and even 6 hours after dosing. Even more, the researchers reported no adverse effects on the patients who took place in the study.

It has also been found (*Lakhan et al., Nutrition Journal. 2008; 7:1*) that bipolar patients also produce high levels of vanadium. This is problematic, because high levels of vanadium can lead to depression. However, vitamin C has been shown to protect the body from problems caused by excess vanadium. In fact, a double-blind, placebo controlled study showed that a single 3 gram dose of vitamin C has the ability to decrease manic symptoms. Combining essential vitamin supplements with the body's natural supply of lithium can make great progress in helping with depression and manic symptoms for those living with bipolar disorder.

Though vitamin C's benefits are discussed more in depth, vitamin B and D are also central to a well-functioning body. Be sure to take extra vitamins when needed to keep your body at healthy levels. However, when taking vitamins for certain deficiencies, it is important to make sure you are only taking as much as you need. It is possible to overdose or abuse vitamins, and if you take too much, it can lead to problems. For instance, too much vitamin C can increase the risk of both kidney stones and diarrhea. Vitamin D on the other hand, may cause some allergic reactions or build up calcium on arteries. Cholesterol changes can also occur. However, these side effects can be easily omitted by making sure you stick to the set doses. Never go overboard when it comes to vitamins, simply take what you need in order to help battle any deficiencies you may be experiencing.

Sources: *Rakofsky et al., Depression and Anxiety. 2014; 31:379*
Lakhan et al., Nutrition Journal. 2008; 7:1

BIPOLAR DISORDER:
35 OUTSIDE OF THE BOX TIPS TO MANAGE BIPOLAR DISORDER

126

35. Yoga

Yoga, the final treatment we will explore, has been touched upon in previous sections. This is because it serves as a blending of different forms, such as tai chi and meditation. As a result, yoga is a good ending point due to the fact that it is a practice which incorporates the whole body along with the mind. The central benefits of yoga are most typically associated with calming or relaxing techniques, but it can be used as a form of low-impact exercise as well. Though this wide range of effects, it is a good way to help with bipolar disorder.

Yoga is a practice built from several different parts, with each part playing a key role in the overall method. On the surface, yoga is focused around relaxation and inner peace. This is most commonly achieved through a combination of poses and breathing exercises. Each of these help you move toward a state of relaxation. The poses and stretching in yoga help relax your body, while the breathing and meditative aspect will help to relax your mind.

In order to achieve the best results when practicing yoga, there are three main components that you want to focus on. These components are posture, breathing exercises and meditation. Posture is important in helping you with the poses, which benefits your body through exercise. However, breathing exercises are the most important aspect of this practice. When using yoga for bipolar disorder you want it to serves as a stress reducer. In addition, it also serves as a good source of emotional regulation. Controlled breathing, which is what happens during the breathing exercises, affects both of these, and will give you the best results in terms of relaxation. For this reason, controlled breathing is considered to be one of the most therapeutic components of yoga. In addition, yoga may also play some roles in your bodily functions as well. It has been shown to activate vagus afferents to autonomic neuroendocrine and limbic circuits with positive impact on both emotion regulation and stress reponsivity. All of these are beneficial bodily functions.

When working at a physiological level, yoga also has mood-influencing benefits as well. These stem from decreasing sympathetic nervous system activity, increasing parasympathetic activity, and causing monoamine changes. In some small trials, it was also shown to alleviate depression, especially when used on those who were living with bipolar disorder. However, as of now there is no conclusive evidence that links yoga to the direct treatment of bipolar disorder. Still, its ability to treat depression makes it a very reasonable method to use.

The side effects that come from yoga are usually related to the physical fitness that naturally comes with the practice. This refers to elements such as natural soreness or any pain that can come from being active. Even a low-impact exercise such as yoga can cause some stress on the body. In terms of the mental, meditation-induced mania or psychosis has been reported in rare instances. Artery occlusion and lotus neuropathy (a sciatic neuropathy due to modified lotus position) have also been seen, but these are also quite rare. Yoga, like many treatments, can be very helpful. However, it is just one example of the ways you can deal with bipolar disorder. Hopefully, this guide will help to lead you towards a treatment that works best for you.

Sources: *Ravindran et al., Journal of Affective Disorders. 2013; 150:707*

www.ingramcontent.com/pod-product-compliance
Lightning Source LLC
Chambersburg PA
CBHW050351280326
41933CB00010BA/1416

* 9 7 8 1 6 1 9 4 9 4 6 8 8 *